GREATEST EVER

Wok & Stir-Fry

This is a Papplewick Press Book
First published in 2002

Papplewick Press
Unit 5 Bestwood Business Park
Bestwood Village
Nottingham NG6 8AN, UK

ISBN: 0-75259-225-4

Printed in Dubai

Produced by The Bridgewater Book Company Ltd

NOTE

This book uses metric and imperial measurements. Follow the same units
of measurement throughout; do not mix metric and imperial.
All spoon measurements are level: teaspoons are assumed to be 5 ml,
and tablespoons are assumed to be 15 ml. Unless otherwise stated,
milk is assumed to be full fat, eggs and individual vegetables such as potatoes
are medium, and pepper is freshly ground black pepper.

The times given for each recipe are an approximate guide only because the
preparation times may differ according to the techniques used by different
people and the cooking times may vary as a result of the type of oven used.

Recipes using raw or very lightly cooked eggs should be
avoided by infants, the elderly, pregnant women, convalescents, and anyone
suffering from an illness.

Contents

Introduction

One of the quickest, easiest and most versatile methods of cooking is to stir-fry in a wok. It takes only a few minutes to assemble the ingredients — a selection of vegetables, to which may be added meat, fish, seafood, tofu, nuts, rice or noodles. The possibilities are endless for ringing the changes with different oils, seasonings and sauces, and the result is a colourful, delicious, healthy meal.

Although the wok can be used for steaming and deep-frying, its main use is for stir-frying. As it cooks, the food is tossed and turned with long bamboo chopsticks, a wok scoop or spatula.

Some foods need a slightly longer cooking time than others and, for this reason, stir-frying is often done in stages. This also allows the individual ingredients to retain their distinct flavours. As they cook, the foods are removed from the wok, but they are always mixed once everything is cooked, and served as a whole dish.

There is plenty of scope for creativity when choosing ingredients, even for the simplest stir-fry. A combination of onions, carrots, peppers (green, red, yellow and orange), broccoli and mangetout will provide the basis for a colourful dish. Add beansprouts at the end of cooking and toss quickly for texture, or some canned water chestnuts, which add a delicious crunch. A few cashew nuts or almonds, some cubed tofu or boneless chicken, or a handful of prawns provide protein, while adding some pre-cooked rice or noodles makes a gutsy stir-fry. A ready-made sauce – perhaps oyster or yellow bean – will finish off the dish. Ginger, garlic and chillies are wonderful for flavouring stir-fries.

Chillies come in a wide variety, ranging in heat from very mild to fiery hot. The Thai's favour the small red or green 'bird-eye' chillies, which are very fiery, and their curries are flavoured with ferociously hot chilli pastes. Crushed dried chillies are also useful for seasoning. Some of the 'kick' can be taken out of a hot chilli by removing the seeds and membranes. Cut fresh chillies in half, and scrape out the seeds with the point of a knife. Cut off the end of dried chillies and shake out the seeds. Always wash your hands after handling chillies!

Basic Recipes

Fresh Chicken Stock

MAKES 1.7 LITRES/3 PINTS

1 kg/2 lb 4 oz chicken, skinned

2 celery sticks

1 onion

2 carrots

1 garlic clove

few fresh parsley sprigs

2 litres/3½ pints water

salt and pepper

1 Put all the ingredients into a large saucepan.

2 Bring to the boil. Skim away any surface scum with a large flat spoon. Reduce the heat to a gentle simmer, partially cover, and cook for 2 hours. Leave to cool.

3 Line a sieve with clean muslin and place over a large jug or bowl. Pour the stock through the sieve. The cooked chicken can be used in another recipe. Discard the other solids. Cover the stock and chill in the refrigerator.

4 Skim away any fat that forms before using. Store in the refrigerator for 3–4 days, until required, or freeze in small batches.

Fresh Fish Stock

MAKES 1.7 LITRES/3 PINTS

1 head of a cod or salmon, etc, plus the trimmings, skin and bones or just the trimmings, skin and bones

1–2 onions, sliced

1 carrot, sliced

1–2 celery sticks, sliced

good squeeze of lemon juice

1 bouquet garni or 2 fresh or dried bay leaves

1 Wash the fish head and trimmings and place in a saucepan. Cover with water and bring to the boil.

2 Skim away any surface scum with a large flat spoon, then add the remaining ingredients. Cover and simmer for about 30 minutes.

3 Strain and cool. Store in the refrigerator and use within 2 days.

Cornflour Paste

Cornflour paste is made by mixing 1 part cornflour with about 1½ parts of cold water. Stir until smooth. The paste is used to thicken sauces.

Fresh Vegetable Stock

This can be kept chilled for up to three days or frozen for up to three months. Salt is not added when cooking the stock: it is better to season it according to the dish in which it its to be used.

MAKES 1.5 LITRES/2¾ PINTS

250 g/9 oz shallots

1 large carrot, diced

1 celery stick, chopped

½ fennel bulb

1 garlic clove

1 bay leaf

a few fresh parsley and tarragon sprigs

2 litres/ 3½ pints water

pepper

1 Put all the ingredients in a large saucepan and bring to the boil.

2 Skim away any surface scum with a large flat spoon. Reduce the heat to a gentle simmer, partially cover and cook for 45 minutes. Remove from the heat and allow to cool.

3 Line a sieve with clean muslin and put over a large jug or bowl. Pour the stock through the sieve. Discard the herbs and vegetables.

4 Cover and store in the refrigerator for up to 3 days, or freeze in small batches.

Fresh Coconut Milk

To make it from fresh grated coconut, place about 250 g/9 oz grated coconut in a bowl, pour over about 600 ml/1 pint of boiling water to just cover and leave to stand for 1 hour. Strain through muslin, squeezing hard to extract as much 'thick' milk as possible. If you require coconut cream, leave to stand, then skim the 'cream' from the surface for use. Unsweetened desiccated coconut can also be used in the same quantities.

Soups & Starters

Soup is indispensable at Asian tables, especially in China, Japan, Korea and South East Asia. It is generally eaten part way through a main meal to clear the palate for further dishes. There are many different types of delicious soups, both thick and thin and, of course, the clear soups which are often served with wontons or dumplings in them.

Starters or snacks are drier foods in general; the spring roll is a well-known Chinese snack and these come in many variations and shapes across the Far East. Other delights are wrapped in pastry, bread and rice paper or are skewered for ease of eating; vegetables, fish and meat are also deep-fried for a crispy coating. These dishes are served as starters in Westernized restaurants to animate the taste buds for the main course.

spicy thai soup with prawns

serves four

2 tbsp tamarind paste

4 fresh red chillies, deseeded and
very finely chopped

2 cloves garlic, crushed

2 tsp finely chopped fresh
root ginger

4 tbsp Thai fish sauce

2 tbsp palm sugar or
caster sugar

1.2 litres/2 pints fish stock

8 kaffir lime leaves

100 g/3½ oz carrots, sliced thinly

350 g/12 oz sweet potato, diced

100 g/3½ oz baby corn cobs, halved

3 tbsp roughly chopped
fresh coriander

100 g/3½ oz cherry
tomatoes, halved

225 g/8 oz fan-tail prawns

1 Place the tamarind paste, red chillies, garlic, ginger, fish sauce, sugar and fish stock in a preheated wok or large, heavy-based frying pan. Roughly tear the lime leaves and add to the wok. Bring to the boil, stirring constantly to blend the flavours.

2 Reduce the heat and add the carrots, sweet potato and baby corn cobs to the mixture in the wok.

3 Leave the soup to simmer, uncovered, for about 10 minutes, or until the vegetables are just tender.

4 Stir the coriander, cherry tomatoes and prawns into the soup and heat through for 5 minutes.

5 Transfer the soup to a warm soup tureen or individual serving bowls and serve hot.

COOK'S TIP

Thai ginger or galangal
is a member of the ginger family,
but it is yellow in colour with
pink sprouts. The flavour
is aromatic and less pungent
than ginger.

thai-style seafood soup

serves four

1.2 litres/2 pints fish stock

1 lemon grass stalk,
  split lengthways

pared rind of ½ lime or 1 kaffir
  lime leaf

2.5-cm/1-inch piece of fresh root
  ginger, sliced

¼ tsp chilli purée

4–6 spring onions

200 g/7 oz large or medium raw
  prawns, peeled and deveined

250 g/9 oz scallops (about 16–20)

2 tbsp fresh coriander leaves

salt

finely chopped red pepper or fresh
  red chilli rings, to garnish

VARIATION

Substitute very small baby
leeks, slivered or sliced thinly
diagonally, for the spring onions.
Include the green parts.

1 Put the stock in a wok or pan with the lemon grass, lime rind or lime leaf, ginger and chilli purée. Bring just to the boil, reduce the heat, cover and simmer for 10–15 minutes.

2 Cut the spring onions in half lengthways, then slice them crossways very thinly. Cut the prawns almost in half lengthways, keeping their tails intact, reserve.

3 Strain the stock, return to the wok or pan and bring to a simmer, with bubbles rising at the edges and the surface trembling. Add the spring onions and cook for 2–3 minutes. Taste the soup and season with salt, if necessary, and stir in a little more chilli purée if wished.

4 Add the scallops and prawns and poach for about 1 minute, until they turn opaque and the prawns curl.

5 Add the coriander leaves, ladle the soup into warmed bowls and garnish with red pepper or chillies.

crab & sweetcorn soup

serves four

1 tbsp sunflower oil

1 tsp Chinese five-spice powder

225 g/8 oz carrots, cut into sticks

150 g/5½ oz drained canned or
    frozen sweetcorn

75 g/2¾ oz peas

6 spring onions, trimmed and sliced

1 fresh red chilli, deseeded and very
    thinly sliced

400 g/14 oz canned white crab
    meat, drained

175 g/6 oz egg noodles

1.7 litres/3 pints fish stock

3 tbsp light soy sauce

1 Heat the sunflower oil in a large preheated wok or heavy-based frying pan.

2 Add the Chinese five-spice powder, carrots, sweetcorn, peas, spring onions and red chilli to the wok and cook for about 5 minutes, stirring constantly.

3 Add the crab meat to the wok or frying pan and gently stir-fry the mixture over a meedium heat for about 1 minute, making sure that the crab meat is evenly distributed.

4 Roughly break up the egg noodles and add to the wok.

5 Pour the fish stock and soy sauce into the mixture in the wok and bring to the boil.

6 Cover the wok or frying pan and leave the soup to simmer for 5 minutes.

7 Stir once more, then ladle the soup into a warm soup tureen or individual serving bowls and serve at once.

coconut & crab soup

serves four

1 tbsp groundnut oil

2 tbsp Thai red curry paste

1 red pepper, deseeded and sliced

600 ml/1 pint coconut milk

600 ml/1 pint fish stock

2 tbsp Thai fish sauce

225 g/8 oz drained canned or fresh
   white crab meat

225 g/8 oz fresh or thawed frozen
   crab claws

2 tbsp chopped fresh coriander

3 spring onions, trimmed and sliced

COOK'S TIP

Clean the wok after use by
washing it with water, using a
mild detergent if necessary, and
a soft cloth or brush. Do not
scrub or use any abrasive cleaner,
as this will scratch the surface.
Dry thoroughly, then wipe the
surface all over with a little
oil to protect the surface.

1 Heat the groundnut oil in a large preheated wok.

2 Add the red curry paste and red pepper to the wok and stir-fry for 1 minute.

3 Add the coconut milk, fish stock and fish sauce and bring to the boil.

4 Add the crab meat, crab claws, coriander and spring onions to the wok.

5 Stir the mixture well and heat thoroughly for 2–3 minutes, or until everything is warmed through.

6 Transfer the soup to warm bowls and serve hot.

chilli fish soup

serves four

15 g/½ oz Chinese
   dried mushrooms

2 tbsp sunflower oil

1 onion, sliced

100 g/3½ oz mangetout

100 g/3½ oz bamboo shoots

3 tbsp sweet chilli sauce

1.2 litres/2 pints fish or
   vegetable stock

3 tbsp light soy sauce

2 tbsp chopped fresh coriander, plus
   extra to garnish

450 g/1 lb cod fillet, skinned
   and cubed

COOK'S TIP

There are many different varieties
of dried mushrooms, but shiitake
are best. They are quite
expensive, but a small amount
will go a long way.

1 Place the mushrooms in a large bowl. Pour over enough boiling water to cover and leave to stand for 5 minutes. Drain the mushrooms thoroughly in a colander. Using a sharp knife, roughly chop them.

2 Heat the sunflower oil in a preheated wok or large frying pan. Add the sliced onion to the wok and stir-fry over a medium heat for 5 minutes, or until softened.

3 Add the mangetout, bamboo shoots, chilli sauce, stock and soy sauce to the wok and bring to the boil.

4 Add the coriander and cod and leave to simmer for 5 minutes, or until the fish is cooked through.

5 Transfer the soup to warm bowls, garnish with extra coriander, if wished, and serve hot.

hot & sour mushroom soup

serves four

2 tbsp tamarind paste

4 fresh red chillies, deseeded and
   very finely chopped

2 garlic cloves, crushed

2 tsp finely chopped fresh
   root ginger

4 tbsp Thai fish sauce

2 tbsp palm sugar or
   caster sugar

8 kaffir lime leaves, torn roughly

1.2 litres/2 pints vegetable stock

100 g/3½ oz carrots, sliced thinly

225 g/8 oz button
   mushrooms, halved

350 g/12 oz shredded
   white cabbage

100 g/3½ oz fine green
   beans, halved

3 tbsp roughly chopped
   fresh coriander

100 g/3½ oz cherry
   tomatoes, halved

1 Place the tamarind paste, chillies,
   garlic, ginger, fish sauce, sugar,
lime leaves and vegetable stock in a
large preheated wok or heavy-based
frying pan. Bring the mixture to the
boil, stirring occasionally.

2 Reduce the heat and add
   the carrots, mushrooms, white
cabbage and green beans. Leave
the soup to simmer, uncovered, for
about 10 minutes, or until the
vegetables are tender, but not soft.

3 Stir the fresh coriander and
   cherry tomatoes into the mixture
in the wok and heat through for
another 5 minutes.

4 Transfer the soup to a warm
   tureen or individual serving
bowls and serve immediately.

COOK'S TIP

Tamarind is the dried fruit of the
tamarind tree. Sold as a pulp or
paste, it is used to give a special
sweet and sour flavour to
Oriental dishes.

spicy chicken noodle soup

serves four

2 tbsp tamarind paste

4 fresh red chillies, deseeded and
finely chopped

2 cloves garlic, crushed

2 tsp finely chopped fresh
root ginger

4 tbsp Thai fish sauce

2 tbsp palm or caster sugar

8 kaffir lime leaves, torn roughly

1.2 litres/2 pints chicken stock

350 g/12 oz skinless boneless
chicken breast portions

100 g/3½ oz carrots, sliced thinly

350 g/12 oz sweet potato, diced

100 g/3½ oz baby corn cobs, halved

3 tbsp roughly chopped fresh
coriander, plus extra to garnish

100 g/3½ oz cherry
tomatoes, halved

150 g/5½ oz flat rice noodles

ground black pepper to garnish

1 Preheat a large wok or frying pan. Place the tamarind paste, chillies, garlic, ginger, fish sauce, sugar, lime leaves and chicken stock in the wok and bring to the boil, stirring constantly. Reduce the heat and cook for about 5 minutes.

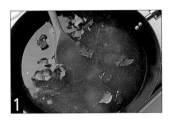

2 Using a sharp knife, thinly slice the chicken. Add the chicken to the wok and cook for a further 5 minutes, stirring the mixture well.

3 Reduce the heat and add the carrots, sweet potato and baby corn cobs to the wok. Leave to simmer, uncovered, for 5 minutes, or until the vegetables are just tender and the chicken is completely cooked through.

4 Stir in the chopped fresh coriander, cherry tomatoes and flat rice noodles.

5 Leave the soup to simmer for about 5 minutes, or until the noodles are tender.

6 Garnish the spicy chicken noodle soup with chopped fresh coriander and pepper, serve hot.

aubergine & mushroom-stuffed omelette

serves four

3 tbsp vegetable oil

1 garlic clove, chopped finely

1 small onion, chopped finely

1 small aubergine, diced

½ small green pepper, deseeded
    and chopped

1 tomato, diced

1 large dried Chinese black
    mushroom, soaked, drained
    and sliced

1 tbsp light soy sauce

½ tsp sugar

¼ tsp ground black pepper

2 large eggs

salad leaves, tomato wedges and
    cucumber sticks, to garnish

1 Heat half the oil in a preheated wok and cook the garlic for 30 seconds. Add the onion and aubergine and stir-fry until golden.

COOK'S TIP

If you heat the pan thoroughly before adding the oil, and heat the oil before adding the ingredients, they will not stick to the pan.

2 Add the green pepper and stir-fry for a further minute. Stir in the tomato, mushroom, soy sauce, sugar and pepper. Remove from the pan and keep hot.

3 Beat the eggs lightly. Heat the remaining oil, swirling to coat the pan. Pour in the eggs and swirl to set around the pan. When the egg is set, spoon the filling into the centre. Fold in the sides of the omelette to make a neat, square parcel.

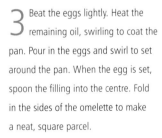

4 Slide the omelette carefully on to a warmed dish and then garnish it with a selection of salad leaves and some tomato wedges and cucumber slices. Serve the omelette hot.

thai-style spicy sweetcorn fritters

serves four

225 g/8 oz drained canned or
frozen sweetcorn kernels

2 fresh red chillies, deseeded and
finely chopped

2 garlic cloves, crushed

10 kaffir lime leaves, chopped finely

2 tbsp chopped fresh coriander

1 large egg

75 g/2¾ oz polenta

100 g/3½ oz fine green beans,
sliced thinly

groundnut oil, for frying

COOK'S TIP

Kaffir lime leaves are dark
green, glossy leaves that have
a lemony-lime flavour. They can
be bought from specialist Asian
stores either fresh or dried.

1 Place the sweetcorn, chillies,
garlic, lime leaves, coriander, egg
and polenta in a large mixing bowl,
and stir to mix.

2 Add the green beans to the
ingredients in the bowl and mix
well, using a wooden spoon.

3 Divide the mixture into small,
even-size balls. Flatten the balls
of mixture between the palms of your
hands to form rounds.

4 Heat a little groundnut oil in a
preheated wok or large frying
pan until really hot. Cook the fritters, in
batches, until brown and crispy on the
outside, turning occasionally.

5 Leave the fritters to drain on
absorbent kitchen paper while
frying the remaining fritters.

6 Using a fish slice, transfer the
drained fritters to warm serving
plates and serve immediately.

vegetable spring rolls

serves four

225 g/8 oz carrots

1 red pepper

1 tbsp sunflower oil, plus extra
    for frying

75 g/2¾ oz beansprouts

finely grated rind and juice of 1 lime

1 fresh red chilli, deseeded and
    finely chopped

1 tbsp light soy sauce

½ tsp arrowroot

2 tbsp chopped fresh coriander

8 sheets filo pastry

2 tbsp butter

2 tsp sesame oil

TO SERVE

spring onion tassels

chilli sauce

1 Using a sharp knife, cut the carrots into thin sticks. Deseed the pepper and cut into thin slices.

2 Heat the sunflower oil in a large preheated wok.

3 Add the carrot, red pepper and beansprouts and cook, stirring, for 2 minutes, or until softened. Remove the wok from the heat and toss in the lime rind and juice, and the red chilli.

4 Mix the soy sauce with the arrowroot to a smooth paste. Stir the mixture into the wok, return to the heat and cook for 2 minutes, or until the juices thicken.

5 Add the chopped fresh coriander to the wok and mix well, then remove the wok from the heat.

6 Lay the sheets of filo pastry out on a board. Melt the butter with the sesame oil and brush each sheet with the mixture.

7 Spoon a little of the vegetable filling on to the top of each sheet, fold over each long side, and roll up.

8 Add a little oil to the wok and cook the spring rolls, in batches, for 2–3 minutes, or until crisp and golden brown.

9 Transfer the spring rolls to a serving dish, garnish with the spring onion tassels and serve hot with chilli dipping sauce.

spicy chicken livers with pak choi

serves four

350 g/12 oz chicken livers

2 tbsp sunflower oil

1 fresh red chilli, deseeded
    and chopped

1 tsp grated fresh root ginger

2 garlic cloves, crushed

2 tbsp tomato ketchup

3 tbsp dry sherry

3 tbsp light soy sauce

1 tsp cornflour

450 g/1 lb pak choi

egg noodles, to serve

1 Using a sharp knife, trim the fat from the chicken livers and slice them into small pieces.

2 Heat the oil in a preheated wok. Add the chicken liver pieces and stir-fry for 2–3 minutes.

3 Add the chilli, ginger and garlic and stir-fry for about 1 minute.

4 Mix together the tomato ketchup, sherry, soy sauce and cornflour in a small bowl and reserve.

5 Add the pak choi to the wok and stir-fry until it just wilts.

6 Add the reserved tomato ketchup mixture to the wok and cook, stirring to mix, until the juices are just starting to bubble.

7 Transfer to serving bowls and serve hot with noodles.

crispy seaweed

serves four

1 kg/2 lb 4 oz pak choi

850 ml/1½ pints groundnut oil, for
   deep-frying

1 tsp salt

1 tbsp caster sugar

2½ tbsp toasted pine kernels

1 Rinse the pak choi leaves under cold running water and then pat them dry thoroughly with absorbent kitchen paper.

2 Discarding any tough outer leaves, roll each pak choi leaf up, then slice through thinly so that the leaves are finely shredded. Alternatively, use a food processor to shred the pak choi.

3 Heat the groundnut oil in a large wok or heavy-based frying pan.

4 Carefully add the shredded pak choi leaves to the wok or frying pan and fry for about 30 seconds, or until they shrivel up and become crispy (you will probably need to do this in several batches, depending on the size of your wok).

5 Remove the crispy 'seaweed' from the wok with a slotted spoon and drain on absorbent kitchen paper.

6 Transfer the crispy seaweed to a large bowl and toss with the salt, sugar and pine kernels. Serve immediately on warm serving plates.

chicken balls with dipping sauce

serves four

2 large skinless, boneless chicken
    breast portions

3 tbsp vegetable oil

2 shallots, chopped finely

½ celery stick, chopped finely

1 garlic clove, crushed

2 tbsp light soy sauce

1 small egg, beaten lightly

1 bunch of spring onions

salt and pepper

spring onion tassels, to garnish

DIPPING SAUCE

3 tbsp dark soy sauce

1 tbsp rice wine

1 tsp sesame seeds

1 Cut the chicken into 2-cm/¾-inch pieces. Heat half of the oil in a preheated wok or frying pan and stir-fry the chicken over a high heat for about 2–3 minutes, until golden. Remove from the wok or pan with a slotted spoon and reserve.

2 Add the shallots, celery and garlic to the wok or pan and stir-fry for 1–2 minutes, until softened.

3 Place the chicken, shallots, celery and garlic in a food processor and process until finely minced. Add 1 tablespoon of the light soy sauce and just enough egg to make a fairly firm mixture. Season to taste with salt and pepper.

4 Trim the spring onions and cut into 5-cm/2-inch lengths. Make the dipping sauce by mixing together the dark soy sauce, rice wine and sesame seeds in a small serving bowl and reserve.

5 Shape the chicken mixture into 16–18 walnut-size balls. Heat the remaining oil in the wok or frying pan and stir-fry the chicken balls, in small batches, for 4–5 minutes, until golden brown. As each batch is cooked, drain on kitchen paper and keep hot.

6 Add the spring onions to the wok or pan and stir-fry for 1–2 minutes, until they begin to soften, then stir in the remaining light soy sauce. Serve with the chicken balls and the bowl of dipping sauce on a platter, garnished with the spring onion tassels.

prawn parcels

serves four

1 tbsp sunflower oil

1 red pepper, deseeded and
thinly sliced

75 g/2¾ oz beansprouts

finely grated rind and juice of 1 lime

1 fresh red chilli, deseeded and
finely chopped

1 tsp grated fresh root ginger

225 g/8 oz peeled raw prawns

1 tbsp Thai fish sauce

½ tsp arrowroot

2 tbsp chopped fresh coriander

8 sheets filo pastry

2 tbsp butter

2 tsp sesame oil

oil, for frying

spring onion tassels, to garnish

chilli dipping sauce, to serve

1 Heat the sunflower oil in a large preheated wok. Add the red pepper and beansprouts and stir-fry over a medium heat for 2 minutes, or until the vegetables have softened.

2 Remove the wok from the heat and toss in the lime rind and juice, red chilli, ginger and prawns, stirring well.

3 Mix the fish sauce with the arrowroot and stir into the wok. Return the wok to the heat and cook, stirring, for 2 minutes, until the juices thicken. Toss in the coriander and mix.

4 Lay the sheets of filo pastry out on a board. Melt the butter with the sesame oil and brush each pastry sheet with the mixture.

5 Spoon a little of the prawn filling on to the top of each sheet, fold over each end, and roll up to enclose the filling.

6 Heat the oil in a large wok. Cook the parcels, in batches, for 2–3 minutes, or until crisp and golden. Garnish with spring onion tassels and serve hot with a chilli dipping sauce.

crispy chilli & peanut prawns

serves four

450 g/1 lb king prawns, peeled but
  leaving the tails intact
3 tbsp crunchy peanut butter
1 tbsp chilli sauce
10 sheets filo pastry
2 tbsp butter, melted
50 g/1¾ oz fine egg noodles
oil, for frying

1 Using a sharp knife, make a small horizontal slit across the back of each prawn. Press down on the prawns so that they lie flat.

2 Mix together the peanut butter and chilli sauce in a small bowl until well blended. Using a pastry brush, spread a little of the sauce on to each prawn so they are evenly coated.

3 Cut each pastry sheet in half and brush with melted butter.

4 Wrap each prawn in a piece of pastry, tucking the edges under to enclose it fully.

5 Place the fine egg noodles in a bowl, pour over enough boiling water to cover and leave to stand for 5 minutes, or according to the packet instructions. Drain the noodles thoroughly. Use 2–3 cooked noodles to tie around each prawn parcel.

6 Heat the oil in a preheated wok. Cook the prawns, in batches if necessary, for 3–4 minutes, or until golden and crispy.

7 Remove the prawns with a slotted spoon, transfer to kitchen paper and leave to drain. Transfer to serving plates and serve warm.

thai-style fish cakes

serves four

450 g/1 lb cod fillet, skinned

2 tbsp Thai fish sauce

2 fresh red Thai chillies, deseeded
    and finely chopped, plus extra
    for garnish

2 garlic cloves, crushed

10 kaffir lime leaves, chopped finely

2 tbsp chopped fresh coriander

1 large egg

25 g/1 oz plain flour

100 g/3½ oz fine green beans,
    sliced thinly

groundnut oil, for frying

COOK'S TIP

Thai fish sauce is a salty, brown
liquid which is a must for
authentic flavour. It is used
to salt dishes, but is milder
in flavour than soy sauce. It
is available from Asian food
stores or health food shops.

1 Using a sharp knife, roughly cut the cod fillets into bite-size pieces.

2 Place the cod pieces in a food processor together with the fish sauce, chillies, garlic, lime leaves, coriander, egg and plain flour. Process until finely chopped and turn out into a large mixing bowl.

3 Add the green beans to the cod mixture and mix.

4 Divide the mixture into small balls. Flatten the balls between the palms of your hands to form rounds.

5 Heat a little oil in a preheated wok. Fry the fish cakes on both sides until brown and crispy on the outside and cooked through.

6 Transfer the fish cakes to serving plates and serve hot, garnished with fresh, whole red chillies.

prawn omelette

serves four

3 tbsp sunflower oil

2 leeks, trimmed and sliced

350 g/12 oz peeled raw
    tiger prawns

4 tbsp cornflour

1 tsp salt

175 g/6 oz mushrooms, sliced

175 g/6 oz beansprouts

6 eggs

deep-fried leeks, to
    garnish (optional)

1 Heat the sunflower oil in a preheated wok or large frying pan. Add the sliced leeks and stir-fry for 3 minutes.

2 Rinse the prawns under cold running water and then pat them dry with kitchen paper.

3 Mix together the cornflour and salt in a large bowl.

4 Add the prawns to the cornflour and salt mixture and toss to coat all over.

5 Add the prawns to the wok or frying pan and stir-fry for 2 minutes, or until the prawns are almost cooked through.

6 Add the sliced mushrooms and beansprouts to the wok and stir-fry for a further 2 minutes.

7 Beat the eggs with 3 tablespoons of cold water. Pour the egg mixture into the wok and cook until the egg sets, carefully turning over once. Turn the omelette out on to a clean board, divide it into 4 and serve immediately, garnished with deep-fried leeks (if using).

sesame prawn toasts

serves four

225 g/8 oz peeled cooked prawns

1 spring onion

¼ tsp salt

1 tsp light soy sauce

1 tbsp cornflour

1 egg white, beaten

3 thin slices white bread,
  crusts removed

4 tbsp sesame seeds

vegetable oil, for deep-frying

COOK'S TIP

Fry the triangles in 2 batches,
keeping the first batch warm
while you cook the second, to
prevent them from sticking
together and overcooking.

1 Put the prawns and spring onion
in a food processor and process
until finely minced. Alternatively, chop
them very finely. Transfer to a bowl
and stir in the salt, soy sauce, cornflour
and egg white.

2 Spread the mixture on to one side
of each slice of bread. Spread the
sesame seeds on top of the mixture,
pressing down well.

3 Cut each slice into 4 equal
triangles or strips.

4 Heat the oil for deep-frying in
a wok until almost smoking.
Carefully place the triangles in the oil,
coated side down, and cook for 2–3
minutes, until golden brown. Remove
with a slotted spoon and drain on
kitchen paper. Serve hot.

salt & pepper prawns

serves four

2 tsp salt

1 tsp black pepper

2 tsp Sezhuan peppercorns

1 tsp sugar

450 g/1 lb peeled raw tiger prawns

2 tbsp groundnut oil

1 fresh red chilli, deseeded and
   finely chopped

1 tsp grated fresh root ginger

3 garlic cloves, crushed

spring onions, sliced, to garnish

prawn crackers, to serve

COOK'S TIP

Tiger prawns are widely
available and have a lovely
meaty texture. If using cooked
tiger prawns, add them with the
salt and pepper mixture in step
5 – if the cooked prawns are
added any earlier, they will
toughen up and be inedible.

1 Grind the salt, black pepper and
Sezhuan peppercorns with a
pestle and mortar.

2 Mix the salt and pepper mixture
with the sugar and reserve
until required.

3 Rinse the tiger prawns under cold
running water and pat dry with
kitchen paper.

4 Heat the oil in a preheated wok
or large frying pan.

5 Add the prawns, chopped red
chilli, ginger and garlic to the
wok or frying pan and stir-fry for
4–5 minutes, or until the prawns are
cooked through.

6 Add the salt and pepper mixture
to the wok and stir-fry for
1 minute, stirring constantly so it does
not burn on the base of the wok.

7 Transfer the prawns to warm
serving bowls and garnish with
spring onions. Serve immediately with
prawn crackers.

vegetarian spring rolls

serves four

25 g/1 oz fine cellophane noodles

2 tbsp groundnut oil

2 garlic cloves, crushed

½ tsp grated fresh root ginger

55 g/2 oz oyster mushrooms,
    sliced thinly

2 spring onions, chopped finely

50 g/1¾ oz beansprouts

1 small carrot, shredded finely

½ tsp sesame oil

1 tbsp light soy sauce

1 tbsp Chinese rice wine or
    dry sherry

¼ tsp pepper

1 tbsp chopped fresh coriander

1 tbsp chopped fresh mint

24 spring-roll wrappers

½ tsp cornflour

groundnut oil, for deep-frying

fresh mint sprigs, to garnish

dipping sauce, to serve

1 Place the noodles in a heatproof bowl, pour over enough boiling water to cover and leave them to stand for 4 minutes. Drain, rinse in cold water, then drain again. Cut or snip the noodles into 5-cm/2-inch lengths.

2 Heat the groundnut oil in a preheated wok or wide pan over a high heat. Add the garlic, ginger, oyster mushrooms, spring onions, beansprouts and carrot and stir-fry for about 1 minute, until just softened.

3 Stir in the sesame oil, soy sauce, rice wine or sherry, pepper, chopped coriander and mint, then remove the wok or pan from the heat. Stir in the rice noodles.

4 Arrange the spring-roll wrappers on a work surface, pointing diagonally. Mix the cornflour with 1 tablespoon water to a smooth paste and brush the edges of 1 wrapper with it. Spoon a little filling on to the point of the same wrapper.

5 Roll the point of the wrapper over the filling, then fold the side points inwards over the filling. Continue to roll up the wrapper away from you, moistening the tip with a little more cornflour paste to secure the roll.

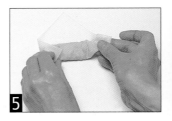

6 Heat the oil in a wok or deep frying pan to 190°C/375°F. Add the rolls, in batches, and deep-fry for 2–3 minutes or until golden and crisp. Drain on kitchen paper and keep warm while you cook the remaining batches. Garnish with the mint sprigs and serve hot with the dipping sauce

seven-spice aubergines

serves four

450 g/1 lb aubergines

1 egg white

3½ tbsp cornflour

1 tbsp seven-spice seasoning

oil, for deep-frying

salt

COOK'S TIP

The best oil to use for deep-frying is groundnut oil which has a high smoke point and mild flavour, so it will neither burn nor taint the food. About 600 ml/1 pint of oil is sufficient.

1 Using a sharp knife, thinly slice the aubergines. Place the slices in a colander, sprinkle with salt and leave to stand for 30 minutes. This will remove all the bitter juices.

2 Rinse the aubergine slices thoroughly and pat dry with absorbent kitchen paper.

3 Place the egg white in a small bowl and whisk with a fork until light and foamy.

4 Using a spoon, mix together the cornflour, 1 teaspoon salt and the seven-spice powder on a plate.

5 Heat the oil for deep-frying in a large preheated wok or a frying pan with a heavy base.

6 Dip the aubergines into the egg white, and then into the cornflour and seven-spice mixture to coat evenly.

7 Deep-fry the coated aubergine slices, in batches, for 5 minutes, or until pale golden and crispy.

8 Transfer the aubergines to kitchen paper and leave to drain. Transfer the seven-spice aubergines to serving plates and serve hot.

Poultry & Meat

Meat is expensive in Far Eastern countries and is eaten in smaller proportions than in the Western world. However, when meat is used, it is done so to its full potential — it is marinated or spiced and mixed with other delicious flavourings to create a wide array of mouthwatering dishes.

In Malaysia, a wide variety of spicy meats is offered, reflecting the many ethnic origins of the population. In China, poultry, lamb, beef or pork are stir-fried or steamed in the wok and mixed with sauces and seasonings such as soy, black bean and oyster sauce. In Japan, meat is usually marinated and quickly stir-fried in a wok over a very high heat or simmered in miso stock. Thai dishes use meat that is leaner and more flavoursome due to its 'free-range' rearing.

coconut chicken curry

serves four

2 tbsp sunflower oil

450 g/1 lb skinless boneless chicken
    thighs or breast portions

150 g/5½ oz okra

1 large onion, sliced

2 cloves garlic, crushed

3 tbsp mild curry paste

300 ml/10 fl oz chicken stock

1 tbsp fresh lemon juice

100 g/3½ oz creamed coconut,
    grated roughly

175 g/6 oz fresh or canned
    pineapple, cubed

150 ml/5 fl oz thick, natural yogurt

2 tbsp chopped fresh coriander

cooked rice, to serve

TO GARNISH

lemon wedges

fresh coriander sprigs

1 Heat the oil in a wok. Cut the chicken into bite-size pieces, add to the wok and stir-fry until evenly browned.

2 Using a sharp knife, trim the okra. Add the onion, garlic and okra to the wok and cook for a further 2–3 minutes, stirring constantly.

3 Mix the curry paste with the chicken stock and lemon juice and pour into the wok. Bring to the boil, cover and leave to simmer for 30 minutes.

4 Stir the grated coconut into the curry and cook for about 5 minutes.

5 Add the pineapple, yogurt and coriander and cook for 2 minutes, stirring. Garnish and serve with cooked rice on warm serving plates.

stir-fried ginger chicken

serves four

2 tbsp sunflower oil

1 onion, sliced

175 g/6 oz carrots, cut
   into matchsticks

1 garlic clove, crushed

350 g/12 oz skinless boneless
   chicken breast portions

2 tbsp grated fresh root ginger

1 tsp ground ginger

4 tbsp sweet sherry

1 tbsp tomato purée

1 tbsp demerara sugar

100 ml/3½ fl oz orange juice

1 tsp cornflour

1 orange, peeled and segmented

snipped fresh chives, to garnish

1 Heat the oil in a large preheated wok. Add the onion, carrots and garlic and stir-fry over a high heat for 3 minutes, or until the vegetables begin to soften.

2 Slice the chicken into thin strips. Add to the wok with the fresh and ground ginger. Stir-fry for a further 10 minutes, or until the chicken is well cooked through and golden in colour.

3 Mix together the sherry, tomato purée, sugar, orange juice and cornflour in a bowl. Stir the mixture into the wok and heat through until the mixture bubbles and the juices start to thicken.

4 Add the orange segments and carefully toss to mix.

5 Transfer the stir-fried chicken to warm individual serving bowls and garnish with snipped fresh chives. Serve immediately.

chicken stir-fry with a trio of peppers

serves four

450 g/1 lb skinless boneless chicken
   breast portions
2 tbsp sunflower oil
1 garlic clove, crushed
1 tbsp cumin seeds
1 tbsp grated fresh root ginger
1 fresh red chilli, deseeded and sliced
1 red pepper, deseeded and sliced
1 green pepper, deseeded
   and sliced
1 yellow pepper, deseeded
   and sliced
100 g/3½ oz beansprouts
350 g/12 oz pak choi or other
   green leaves
2 tbsp sweet chilli sauce
3 tbsp light soy sauce
deep-fried crispy ginger, to garnish
   (see Cook's Tip)
freshly cooked noodles, to serve

1 Using a sharp knife, slice the chicken into thin strips.

2 Heat the oil in a large preheated wok.

3 Add the chicken to the wok and stir-fry for 5 minutes.

4 Add the garlic, cumin seeds, ginger and chilli to the wok, stirring to mix.

5 Add all of the peppers to the wok and stir-fry for a further 5 minutes.

6 Toss in the beansprouts and pak choi together with the sweet chilli sauce and soy sauce and continue to cook until the pak choi leaves start to wilt.

7 Transfer to serving bowls, garnish with ginger (see Cook's Tip) and serve with freshly cooked noodles.

COOK'S TIP

To make the deep-fried crispy ginger garnish, peel and thinly slice a large piece of root ginger, using a sharp knife. Carefully lower the slices of ginger into a wok or small pan of hot oil and cook for about 30 seconds. Remove the deep-fried ginger with a slotted spoon, transfer to sheets of absorbent kitchen paper and leave to drain thoroughly.

sweet & sour chicken with mango

serves four

1 tbsp sunflower oil

6 skinless boneless chicken thighs

1 ripe mango

2 garlic cloves, crushed

225 g/8 oz leeks, shredded

100 g/3½ oz beansprouts

150 ml/5 fl oz mango juice

1 tbsp white wine vinegar

2 tbsp clear honey

2 tbsp tomato ketchup

1 tsp cornflour

1 Heat the sunflower oil in a large preheated wok.

2 Using a sharp knife, cut the chicken into bite-size cubes.

3 Add the chicken to the wok and stir-fry over a high heat for 10 minutes, tossing frequently, until the chicken is cooked through and golden in colour.

4 Meanwhile, peel, stone and slice the mango.

5 Add the garlic, leeks, mango and beansprouts to the wok and stir-fry for a further 2–3 minutes, or until softened.

6 Mix together the mango juice, white wine vinegar, clear honey and tomato ketchup with the cornflour in a measuring jug or bowl.

7 Pour the mango juice and cornflour mixture into the wok and stir-fry for a further 2 minutes, or until the juices start to thicken.

8 Transfer to a warmed serving dish and serve immediately.

chicken & spring green stir-fry

serves four

2 tbsp sunflower oil

450 g/1 lb skinless boneless
chicken breast portions

2 garlic cloves, crushed

1 green pepper

100 g/3½ oz mangetout

6 spring onions, sliced, plus extra to
garnish (optional)

225 g/8 oz spring greens or
cabbage, shredded

160 g/5¾ oz jar yellow bean sauce

50 g/1¾ oz roasted cashew nuts

1 Heat the sunflower oil in a large
preheated wok.

2 Using a sharp knife, slice the
chicken into thin strips.

3 Add the chicken to the wok
together with the garlic. Stir-fry
for about 5 minutes, or until the
chicken is sealed on all sides and
beginning to turn golden.

4 Using a sharp knife, deseed
the green pepper and cut into
thin strips.

5 Add the mangetout, spring
onions, green pepper strips and
spring greens or cabbage to the wok.
Stir-fry for a further 5 minutes, or until
the vegetables are just tender.

6 Stir in the yellow bean sauce and
heat through for about 2 minutes,
or until the mixture starts to bubble.

7 Scatter with the roasted cashew
nuts, then remove the wok from
the heat.

8 Transfer the chicken, spring green
and yellow bean stir-fry to warm
serving plates and garnish with extra
spring onions, if desired. Serve the
stir-fry immediately.

chicken, pepper & orange stir-fry

serves four

3 tbsp sunflower oil

350 g/12 oz skinless boneless
    chicken thighs, cut into thin strips

1 onion, sliced

1 garlic clove, crushed

1 red pepper, deseeded and sliced

85 g/3 oz mangetout

4 tbsp light soy sauce

4 tbsp dry sherry

1 tbsp tomato purée

finely grated rind and juice of
    1 orange

1 tsp cornflour

2 oranges

100 g/3½ oz beansprouts

cooked rice or egg noodles, to serve

COOK'S TIP

Beansprouts are sprouting
mung beans and are a regular
ingredient in Chinese cooking.
They require very little cooking
and may even be eaten
raw, if wished.

---

1 Heat the oil in a large preheated wok. Add the chicken and stir-fry for 2–3 minutes, or until sealed and lightly coloured on all sides.

2 Add the onion, garlic, red pepper and mangetout to the wok. Stir-fry for a further 5 minutes, or until the vegetables are just tender and the chicken is completely cooked through.

3 Mix the soy sauce, sherry, tomato purée, orange rind and juice and the cornflour. Add to the wok and cook, stirring constantly, until the juices start to thicken.

4 Using a sharp knife, peel and segment the oranges. Add the segments to the wok with the beansprouts and heat through for a further 2 minutes.

5 Transfer the stir-fry to warmed individual serving plates and serve immediately with cooked rice or egg noodles.

thai red chicken with cherry tomatoes

serves four

1 tbsp sunflower oil

450 g/1 lb skinless boneless chicken
breast portions

2 garlic cloves, crushed

2 tbsp Thai red curry paste

2 tbsp fresh grated galangal or
root ginger

1 tbsp tamarind paste

4 kaffir lime leaves

225 g/8 oz sweet potato

600 ml/1 pint coconut milk

225 g/8 oz cherry tomatoes, halved

3 tbsp chopped fresh coriander

cooked jasmine or Thai fragrant rice,
to serve

1 Heat the sunflower oil in a large
preheated wok.

2 Thinly slice the chicken. Add the
chicken to the wok and stir-fry for
5 minutes.

3 Add the garlic, curry paste,
galangal or root ginger, tamarind
and lime leaves to the wok and stir-fry
for 1 minute.

4 Using a sharp knife, peel and dice
the sweet potato.

5 Add the coconut milk and sweet
potato to the mixture in the wok
and bring to the boil. Allow to bubble

over a medium heat for 20 minutes,
or until the juices start to thicken
and reduce.

6 Add the cherry tomatoes
and coriander to the curry and
cook for a further 5 minutes, stirring
occasionally. Transfer to serving plates
and serve hot with cooked jasmine
or Thai fragrant rice.

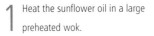

chicken chop suey

serves four

4 tbsp light soy sauce

2 tsp light brown sugar

500 g/1 lb 2 oz skinless, boneless
   chicken breasts

3 tbsp vegetable oil

2 onions, quartered

2 garlic cloves, crushed

350 g/12 oz beansprouts

3 tsp sesame oil

1 tbsp cornflour

3 tbsp water

425 ml/15 fl oz chicken stock

shredded leek, to garnish

1 Mix the soy sauce and sugar together, stirring until the sugar has dissolved.

2 Trim any fat from the chicken and cut into thin strips. Place the meat in a shallow dish and spoon the soy mixture over them, turning to coat. Marinate in the refrigerator for 20 minutes.

3 Heat the oil in a preheated wok and stir-fry the chicken for 2–3 minutes, until golden brown. Add the onions and garlic and cook for a further 2 minutes. Add the beansprouts, cook for 4–5 minutes, add the sesame oil.

4 Mix the cornflour and water to form a smooth paste. Pour the stock into the wok, add the cornflour paste and bring to the boil, stirring until the sauce is thickened and clear. Serve, garnished with shredded leek.

yellow bean chicken

serves four

450 g/1 lb skinless boneless chicken
  breast portions

1 egg white, beaten

1 tbsp cornflour

1 tbsp rice wine vinegar

1 tbsp light soy sauce

1 tsp caster sugar

3 tbsp vegetable oil

1 garlic clove, crushed

1-cm/½-inch piece of fresh root
  ginger, grated

1 green pepper, deseeded and diced

2 large mushrooms, sliced

3 tbsp yellow bean sauce

yellow or green pepper strips,
  to garnish

VARIATION

Black bean sauce would work
equally well with this recipe.
Although this would affect the
appearance of the dish, because
black bean sauce is much
darker in colour, the flavours
would be compatible.

---

1 Trim any fat from the chicken and then cut into the meat into 2.5-cm/ 1-inch cubes.

2 Mix the egg white and cornflour in a shallow bowl. Add the chicken and turn in the mixture to coat. Reserve for 20 minutes.

3 Mix the rice wine vinegar, soy sauce and caster sugar in a bowl.

4 Remove the chicken from the egg white mixture.

5 Heat the oil in a preheated wok, add the chicken and stir-fry for 3–4 minutes, until golden brown. Remove the chicken from the wok with a slotted spoon, drain on kitchen paper and keep warm.

6 Add the garlic, ginger, pepper and mushrooms to the wok and stir-fry for 1–2 minutes.

7 Add the yellow bean sauce and cook for 1 minute. Stir in the vinegar mixture and return the chicken to the wok. Cook for 1–2 minutes and serve hot, garnished with pepper strips.

chicken & beans

serves four

225 g/8 oz dried black-eyed beans,
 soaked overnight and drained

1 tsp salt

2 onions, chopped

2 garlic cloves, crushed

1 tsp ground turmeric

1 tsp ground cumin

1.25 kg/2 lb 12 oz chicken, jointed
 into 8 pieces

1 green pepper, deseeded
 and chopped

2 tbsp vegetable oil

2.5-cm/1-inch piece of fresh root
 ginger, grated

2 tsp coriander seeds

½ tsp fennel seeds

2 tsp garam masala

1 tbsp chopped fresh coriander,
 to garnish

1 Put the dried black-eyed beans into a wok or pan with the salt, onions, garlic, turmeric and cumin. Cover the beans with water, bring to the boil and cook for 15 minutes.

2 Add the chicken and green pepper to the pan and bring to the boil. Reduce the heat and simmer gently for 30 minutes, until the beans are tender and the chicken juices run clear when the thickest parts of the pieces are pierced with a sharp knife or skewer.

3 Heat the oil in a wok or frying pan and fry the ginger, coriander seeds and fennel seeds for 30 seconds.

4 Stir the spices into the chicken and add the garam masala. Simmer gently for a further 5 minutes, garnish with chopped coriander and serve immediately.

braised garlic chicken

serves four

4 garlic cloves, chopped

4 shallots, chopped

2 small fresh red chillies, deseeded
and chopped

1 lemon grass stalk, chopped finely

1 tbsp chopped fresh coriander

1 tsp shrimp paste

½ tsp ground cinnamon

1 tbsp tamarind paste

2 tbsp vegetable oil

8 small chicken joints, such as
drumsticks or thighs

300 ml/10 fl oz chicken stock

1 tbsp Thai fish sauce

1 tbsp smooth peanut butter

4 tbsp toasted peanuts, chopped

salt and pepper

TO SERVE

stir-fried vegetables

freshly cooked noodles

1 Place the garlic, shallots, chillies, lemon grass, coriander and shrimp paste in a mortar and grind with a pestle to an almost smooth paste. Stir in the cinnamon and tamarind paste.

2 Heat the oil in a wok or frying pan. Add the chicken and cook, turning frequently, until golden brown on all sides. Remove with a slotted spoon and keep hot. Tip away any excess fat.

3 Add the garlic paste to the wok or pan and cook over a medium heat, stirring constantly, until lightly browned. Stir in the stock and return the chicken to the wok or pan.

4 Bring to the boil, then cover tightly, lower the heat and simmer, stirring occasionally, for 25–30 minutes, until the chicken is tender and thoroughly cooked. Stir in the fish sauce and peanut butter and simmer gently for a further 10 minutes.

5 Season to taste with salt and pepper and sprinkle the toasted peanuts over the chicken. Serve immediately, with a colourful selection of stir-fried vegetables and freshly cooked noodles.

55

chicken with lemon & sesame seeds

serves four

4 skinless boneless chicken
   breast portions
1 egg white
25 g/1 oz sesame seeds
2 tbsp vegetable oil
1 onion, sliced
1 tbsp demerara sugar
finely grated rind and juice of
   1 lemon
3 tbsp lemon curd
200 g/7 oz can water chestnuts
strips of lemon rind, to garnish
freshly cooked rice, to serve

COOK'S TIP

Water chestnuts are commonly
added to Chinese recipes purely
for their crunchy texture, as
they do not have a great
deal of flavour.

1 Place the chicken portions between 2 sheets of clingfilm and pound with a rolling pin to flatten. Slice the chicken into thin strips.

2 Whisk the egg white until light and foamy.

3 Dip the chicken strips into the egg white, then into the sesame seeds until coated evenly.

4 Heat the vegetable oil in a large preheated wok.

5 Add the onion to the wok and stir-fry until just softened.

6 Add the sesame-coated chicken to the wok and continue stir-frying for 5 minutes, or until the chicken turns golden.

7 Mix together the sugar, lemon rind, lemon juice and the lemon curd and add the mixture to the wok. Allow the lemon mixture to bubble slightly without stirring.

8 Drain the water chestnuts and slice them thinly, using a sharp knife. Add the water chestnuts to the wok and heat through for 2 minutes. Transfer to serving bowls, garnish with lemon rind and serve hot with rice.

chicken with cashews & yellow bean sauce

serves four

450 g/1 lb boneless chicken
   breast portions
2 tbsp vegetable oil
1 red onion, sliced
175 g/6 oz flat mushrooms, sliced
100 g/3½ oz cashew nuts
75 g/2¾ oz jar yellow bean sauce
fresh coriander, to garnish
egg fried rice, to serve

COOK'S TIP
Boneless chicken thighs could be used instead for a more economical dish.

1

3

4

1 Using a sharp knife, remove the excess skin from the chicken if desired. Cut the chicken into small, bite-size chunks.

2 Heat the vegetable oil in a preheated wok.

3 Add the chicken to the wok and stir-fry over a medium heat for 5 minutes.

4 Add the red onion and mushrooms to the wok and continue to stir-fry for a further 5 minutes.

5 Place the cashew nuts on a baking tray and toast under a preheated medium grill until just browning – this brings out their flavour.

6 Toss the toasted cashew nuts into the wok together with the yellow bean sauce. Allow the sauce to bubble for 2–3 minutes.

7 Transfer the stir-fry to warm serving bowls and garnish with fresh coriander. Serve immediately with egg fried rice.

peppered chicken with sugar snap peas

serves four

2 tbsp tomato ketchup

2 tbsp light soy sauce

450 g/1 lb skinless boneless chicken breast portions

2 tbsp crushed mixed peppercorns

2 tbsp sunflower oil

1 red pepper

1 green pepper

175 g/6 oz sugar snap peas

2 tbsp oyster sauce

VARIATION

Use mangetout instead of sugar snap peas, if you prefer.

1 Mix the tomato ketchup with the soy sauce in a bowl.

2 Using a sharp knife, slice the chicken into thin strips. Toss the chicken in the tomato ketchup and soy sauce mixture.

3 Sprinkle the crushed peppercorns on to a plate. Dip the coated chicken in the peppercorns until evenly coated.

4 Heat the sunflower oil in a preheated wok.

5 Add the chicken to the wok and stir-fry for 5 minutes.

6 Deseed and slice the red and green peppers into strips.

7 Add the peppers to the wok together with the sugar snap peas and stir-fry for a further 5 minutes.

8 Add the oyster sauce and allow to bubble for 2 minutes. Transfer to serving bowls and serve immediately.

honey & soy chicken with beansprouts

serves four

2 tbsp clear honey

3 tbsp light soy sauce

1 tsp Chinese five-spice powder

1 tbsp sweet sherry

1 garlic clove, crushed

8 chicken thighs

1 tbsp sunflower oil

1 fresh red chilli

100 g/3½ oz baby corn cobs, halved

8 spring onions, sliced

150 g/5½ oz beansprouts

COOK'S TIP

Chinese five-spice powder is found in most large supermarkets and is a blend of aromatic spices.

1 Mix together the honey, soy sauce, Chinese five-spice powder, sherry and garlic in a large bowl.

2 Using a sharp knife, make 3 slashes in the skin of each chicken thigh. Brush the honey and soy marinade over the chicken thighs, cover and leave to stand for at least 30 minutes.

3 Heat the sunflower oil in a large preheated wok.

4 Add the chicken thighs to the wok and cook over a fairly high heat, turning frequently, for 12–15 minutes, or until the chicken browns and the skin begins to crisp. Remove the chicken with a slotted spoon.

5 Using a sharp knife, deseed and very finely chop the chilli.

6 Add the chilli, corn cobs, spring onions and beansprouts to the wok and stir-fry for 5 minutes.

7 Return the chicken to the wok and mix all of the ingredients together until completely heated through.

8 Transfer to serving plates and serve immediately.

stir-fried chicken with chilli & crispy basil

serves four

8 chicken drumsticks

2 tbsp soy sauce

1 tbsp sunflower oil

1 fresh red chilli

100 g/3½ oz carrots, cut into
  matchsticks

6 celery sticks, cut into matchsticks

3 tbsp sweet chilli sauce

oil, for frying

about 50 fresh basil leaves

freshly cooked noodles, to serve

1 Remove the skin from the chicken drumsticks if desired. Make 3 slashes in each drumstick. Brush the drumsticks with the soy sauce.

2 Heat the sunflower oil in a preheated wok and fry the drumsticks for 20 minutes, turning frequently, until they are cooked through and golden.

3 Deseed and finely chop the chilli. Add the chilli, carrots and celery to the wok and cook for a further 5 minutes. Stir in the chilli sauce, cover and allow to bubble gently while preparing the basil leaves.

4 Heat a little oil in a heavy-based pan. Carefully add the basil leaves – stand well away from the pan and protect your hand with a tea towel, as they may spit a little. Cook the basil leaves for about 30 seconds, or until they begin to curl up but not brown. Leave the leaves to drain on kitchen paper.

5 Transfer the cooked chicken, vegetables and pan juices to a warm serving platter, garnish with the deep-fried crispy basil leaves and serve immediately with freshly cooked rice.

garlic chicken with coriander & lime

serves four

4 large skinless boneless chicken
 breast portions

50 g/1¾ oz garlic butter, softened

3 tbsp chopped fresh coriander

1 tbsp sunflower oil

finely grated rind and juice of
 2 limes

25 g/1 oz palm sugar or
 demerara sugar

fresh coriander, to garnish (optional)

cooked rice, to serve

1 Place each chicken portion
between 2 sheets of clingfilm
and pound with a rolling pin until
flattened to about 1 cm/½ inch thick.

2 Mix together the garlic butter and
coriander and spread over each
flattened chicken piece. Roll up like a
Swiss roll and secure with cocktail sticks.

3 Heat the oil in a wok. Add the
chicken rolls and cook, turning
frequently, for 15–20 minutes, or until
cooked through.

4 Remove the chicken from the wok
and transfer to a board. Cut each
chicken roll into slices.

5 Add the lime rind, juice and sugar
to the wok and heat gently,
stirring, until the sugar has dissolved.
Raise the heat and allow to bubble for
2 minutes.

6 Arrange the chicken on warmed
serving plates and spoon the pan
juices over to serve.

7 Garnish with extra coriander, if
desired, and serve with rice.

thai stir-fried chicken

serves four

3 tbsp groundnut oil

350 g/12 oz skinless boneless
   chicken breast portions, sliced

8 shallots, sliced

2 garlic cloves, chopped finely

2 tsp grated fresh root ginger

1 fresh green chilli, deseeded and
   finely chopped

1 red pepper, deseeded and
   thinly sliced

1 green pepper, deseeded and
   thinly sliced

3 courgettes, sliced thinly

2 tbsp ground almonds

1 tsp ground cinnamon

1 tbsp oyster sauce

20 g/¾ oz creamed coconut, grated

salt and pepper

1 Heat the groundnut oil in a preheated wok or heavy-based frying pan. Add the chicken, season to taste with salt and pepper and stir-fry over a medium heat for about 4 minutes.

2 Add the shallots, garlic, ginger and fresh green chilli and stir-fry for a further 2 minutes.

3 Add the red and green peppers and courgettes and stir-fry for about 1 minute.

4 Stir in the almonds, cinnamon, oyster sauce and creamed coconut and season to taste with salt and pepper. Stir-fry for 1 minute to heat through and then serve immediately.

COOK'S TIP
Creamed coconut is sold in blocks by supermarkets and oriental stores. It is a useful store-cupboard standby because it adds richness and depth of flavour.

chicken & corn sauté

serves four

4 skinless boneless chicken
   breast portions
250 g/9 oz baby corn cobs
250 g/9 oz mangetout
2 tbsp sunflower oil
1 tbsp sherry vinegar
1 tbsp clear honey
1 tbsp light soy sauce
1 tbsp sunflower seeds
pepper
cooked rice or egg noodles, to serve

VARIATION

Rice vinegar or balsamic vinegar
make good substitutes for the
sherry vinegar.

1 Using a sharp knife, slice the
chicken breast portions into long,
thin strips.

2 Cut the baby corn cobs in half
lengthways or slice diagonally
and trim the mangetout.

3 Heat the sunflower oil in a preheated wok or a wide frying pan.

4 Add the chicken and stir-fry over
a fairly high heat for 1 minute.

5 Add the baby corn cobs and
mangetout and stir-fry over a
moderate heat for 5–8 minutes, until
evenly cooked. The vegetables should
still be slightly crunchy.

6 Mix the sherry vinegar, honey and
soy sauce in a small bowl.

7 Stir the vinegar mixture into the
pan with the sunflower seeds.

8 Season to taste with pepper. Cook,
stirring constantly, for 1 minute.

9 Serve the chicken and corn sauté
immediately with cooked rice or
egg noodles.

thai-spiced coriander chicken

serves four

4 skinless boneless chicken
   breast portions

2 garlic cloves, peeled

1 fresh green chilli, deseeded

2-cm/¾-inch piece of fresh
   root ginger

4 tbsp chopped fresh coriander

rind of 1 lime, grated finely

3 tbsp lime juice

2 tbsp light soy sauce

1 tbsp caster sugar

175 ml/6 fl oz coconut milk

TO SERVE

plain boiled rice

cucumber and radish salad

1 Using a sharp knife, cut 3 deep slashes into the skinned side of each chicken breast portion. Place them in a single layer in a wide, non-metallic dish.

2 Put the garlic, chilli, ginger, coriander, lime rind and juice, soy sauce, caster sugar and coconut milk in a food processor and process to a smooth purée.

3 Spread the purée over both sides of the chicken portions, coating them evenly. Cover the dish with clingfilm and leave to marinate in the refrigerator for about 1 hour.

4 Lift the chicken from the marinade, drain off the excess and place in a grill pan. Cook under a preheated grill for 12–15 minutes, until thoroughly and evenly cooked.

5 Meanwhile, place the remaining marinade in a wok or pan and bring to the boil. Reduce the heat and simmer for 3–5 minutes to heat thoroughly. Remove the wok or pan from the heat.

6 Place the chicken breast portions on warmed individual serving plates and pour over the sauce. Serve immediately accompanied with boiled rice and cucumber and radish salad.

chicken & mango stir-fry

serves four

6 skinless boneless chicken thighs

2 tsp grated fresh root ginger

1 garlic clove, crushed

1 small fresh red chilli, deseeded

1 large red pepper, deseeded

4 spring onions

200 g/7 oz mangetout

100 g/3½ oz baby corn cobs

1 large ripe mango

2 tbsp sunflower oil

1 tbsp light soy sauce

3 tbsp rice wine or dry sherry

1 tsp sesame oil

salt and pepper

snipped fresh chives,

   to garnish

1 Cut the chicken into long, thin strips and place in a bowl. Mix the ginger, garlic and chilli, then stir the mixture into the chicken strips to coat them evenly.

2 Slice the pepper thinly, cutting diagonally. Trim and diagonally slice the spring onions. Cut the mangetout and corn cobs in half diagonally. Peel the mango, remove the stone and cut into small chunks.

3 Heat the sunflower oil in a large, preheated wok or heavy-based frying pan over a high heat. Add the chicken and stir-fry for 4–5 minutes, until sealed all over and just turning golden brown. Add the red pepper slices and stir-fry over a medium heat for 4–5 minutes, until softened.

4 Add the spring onions, mangetout and corn cobs and stir-fry for a further minute.

5 Mix the soy sauce, rice wine or sherry and sesame oil and stir the mixture into the wok. Add the mango slices and stir gently for 1 minute, until heated through.

6 Season to taste with salt and pepper, garnish with snipped fresh chives and serve immediately.

duck with baby corn cobs & pineapple

serves four

4 duck breasts

1 tsp Chinese five-spice powder

1 tbsp cornflour

1 tbsp chilli oil

225 g/8 oz baby onions, peeled

2 garlic cloves, crushed

100 g/3½ oz baby corn cobs

175 g/6 oz canned
  pineapple chunks

6 spring onions, sliced

100 g/3½ oz beansprouts

2 tbsp plum sauce

1 Remove any skin from the duck breasts. Cut the duck meat into thin slices.

2 Mix the Chinese five-spice powder and the cornflour in a bowl. Toss the duck slices in the mixture until well coated.

3 Heat the oil in a preheated wok. Stir-fry the duck for 10 minutes, or until just beginning to crispen around the edges. Remove from wok with a slotted spoon and keep warm.

4 Add the onions and garlic to the wok and stir-fry for 5 minutes, or until softened. Add the baby corn cobs and stir-fry for a further 5 minutes. Add the pineapple, spring onions and beansprouts and stir-fry for a further 3–4 minutes. Stir in the plum sauce.

5 Return the cooked duck to the wok and toss until well mixed. Transfer to warm serving dishes and serve hot.

ginger duck with rice

serves four

2 duck breasts, cut diagonally into
thin slices

2–3 tbsp Japanese soy sauce

1 tbsp mirin or medium sherry

2 tsp brown sugar

5-cm/2-inch piece of fresh root
ginger, finely chopped or grated

4 tbsp groundnut oil

2 garlic cloves, crushed

300 g/10½ oz long-grain white or
brown rice

850 ml/1½ pints chicken stock

115 g/4 oz cooked lean ham,
sliced thinly

175 g/6 oz mangetout, cut
diagonally in half

40 g/1½ oz beansprouts, rinsed

8 spring onions, thinly
sliced diagonally

2–3 tbsp chopped fresh coriander

sweet or hot chilli sauce (optional)

1 Put the duck in a shallow bowl
with a tablespoon of soy sauce,
the mirin, half the brown sugar and
one-third of the ginger. Stir to coat
thoroughly and leave to marinate at
room temperature.

2 Heat 2–3 tablespoons groundnut
oil in a large heavy-based pan
over a medium-high heat. Add the
garlic and half the remaining ginger
and stir-fry for about 1 minute, until
fragrant. Add the rice and cook,
stirring, for about 3 minutes, until
translucent and beginning to colour.

3 Add 700 ml/1¼ pints stock and a
teaspoon of soy sauce and bring
to the boil. Reduce the heat to very
low, cover and simmer for 20 minutes,
until the rice is tender and the liquid is
absorbed. Do not uncover the pan, but
remove from the heat and reserve.

4 Heat the remaining groundnut oil
in a large wok. Drain the duck
and gently stir-fry for about 3 minutes,
until just coloured. Add 1 tablespoon
soy sauce and the remaining sugar and
cook for 1 minute. Remove from the
wok, set aside and keep warm.

5 Stir in the ham, mangetout,
beansprouts, spring onions, the
remaining ginger and about half the
coriander. Add about 125 ml/4 fl oz of
the stock and stir-fry for 1 minute, or
until the stock is almost completely
reduced. Fork in the rice and toss. Add
a dash of chilli sauce, if using.

6 To serve, turn into a serving dish,
arrange the duck on top and
sprinkle with the remaining coriander.

duck with mangoes

serves four

2 ripe mangoes

300 ml/10 fl oz chicken stock

2 garlic cloves, crushed

1 tsp grated fresh root ginger

2 large skinless duck breasts,
    225 g/8 oz each

3 tbsp vegetable oil

1 tsp wine vinegar

1 tsp light soy sauce

1 leek, sliced

chopped fresh parsley, to garnish

1 Peel the mangoes and cut the flesh from each side of the stones. Cut the flesh into strips.

2 Put half of the mango pieces and the chicken stock in a food processor and process until smooth. Alternatively, press half of the mangoes through a fine sieve with the back of a spoon and mix with the stock.

3 Rub the garlic and ginger over the duck breasts. Heat the oil in a preheated wok and cook the duck breasts, turning frequently, until sealed. Reserve the oil in the wok and remove the duck.

4 Place the duck breasts on a rack set over a roasting tin and cook in a preheated oven, 220°C/425°F/Gas Mark 7, for about 20 minutes, until the duck is cooked through.

5 Meanwhile, place the mango and chicken stock mixture in a saucepan and add the wine vinegar and light soy sauce.

6 Bring the mixture to the boil and cook over a high heat, stirring constantly, until reduced by half.

7 Heat the oil reserved in the wok and stir-fry the sliced leek and remaining mango for 1 minute. Remove from the wok from the heat, transfer to a serving dish and keep warm until required.

8 Slice the cooked duck breasts neatly and arrange the slices on top of the leek and mango mixture. Pour the sauce over the duck slices, garnish with chopped parsley and serve immediately.

crispy duck with noodles & tamarind

serves four

3 duck breast portions, total weight
about 400 g/14 oz

2 garlic cloves, crushed

1½ tsp chilli paste

1 tbsp clear honey

3 tbsp dark soy sauce

½ tsp Chinese five-spice powder

250 g/9 oz rice stick noodles

1 tsp vegetable oil

1 tsp sesame oil

2 spring onions, sliced

100 g/3½ oz mangetout

2 tbsp tamarind juice

sesame seeds, to garnish

1 Prick the skin of the duck breasts all over with a fork and place them in a deep dish.

2 Mix the garlic, chilli, honey, soy sauce and five-spice powder, then pour over the duck. Turn the duck over to coat it evenly, then cover with clingfilm and leave to marinate in the refrigerator for at least 1 hour.

3 Meanwhile, soak the rice noodles in hot water for 15 minutes, or according to the packet instructions. Drain well.

4 Drain the duck from the marinade and grill on a rack under high heat for about 10 minutes, turning occasionally, until a rich golden brown. Remove with tongs, place on a board and slice thinly.

5 Heat the vegetable and sesame oils in a preheated wok and stir-fry the spring onions and mangetout for 2 minutes. Stir in the reserved marinade and the tamarind juice and bring to the boil.

6 Add the sliced duck and noodles and toss to heat thoroughly. Transfer to warmed serving plates and serve, sprinkled with sesame seeds.

hoisin duck with leek & stir-fried cabbage

serves four

4 duck breasts

350 g/12 oz green cabbage

225 g/8 oz leeks, sliced

finely grated rind of 1 orange

6 tbsp oyster sauce

1 tsp toasted sesame seeds,
    to serve

1 Heat a large wok and dry-fry the duck breasts, with the skin on, for about 5 minutes on each side (you may need to do this in batches).

2 Remove the duck breasts from the wok with tongs and transfer to a clean board.

3 Using a sharp knife, cut the duck breasts into thin slices.

4 Remove and discard all but 1 tablespoon of the fat from the duck left in the wok.

5 Using a sharp knife, finely shred the green cabbage.

6 Add the leeks, green cabbage and orange rind to the wok and stir-fry for about 5 minutes, or until the vegetables have softened.

7 Return the duck to the wok and heat through for 2–3 minutes.

8 Drizzle the oyster sauce over the mixture in the wok, toss well until all the ingredients are mixed and then heat through.

9 Scatter the stir-fry with toasted sesame seeds, transfer to a warm serving dish and serve hot.

stir-fried turkey with cranberry glaze

serves four

450g/1lb boneless turkey breast

2 tbsp sunflower oil

15 g/½ oz stem ginger

50 g/1¾ oz fresh or

frozen cranberries

100 g/3½ oz canned chestnuts

4 tbsp cranberry sauce

3 tbsp light soy sauce

salt and pepper

COOK'S TIP

It is very important that the wok is very hot before you stir-fry. Test by by holding your hand flat about 7.5 cm/3 inches above the base of the interior – you should be able to feel the heat radiating from it.

1 Remove any skin from the turkey breast. Using a sharp knife, thinly slice the turkey breast.

2 Heat the sunflower oil in a large preheated wok or heavy-based frying pan.

3 Add the turkey to the wok or pan and stir-fry for 5 minutes, or until cooked through.

4 Drain off the syrup from the stem ginger. Using a sharp knife, chop the ginger finely.

5 Add the ginger and the cranberries to the wok or frying pan and stir-fry for 2–3 minutes, or until the cranberries have softened.

6 Add the chestnuts, cranberry sauce and soy sauce, season to taste with salt and pepper and allow to bubble for 2–3 minutes.

7 Transfer the glazed turkey stir-fry to individual warm serving dishes and serve immediately.

beef with bamboo shoots & mangetout

350 g/12 oz rump steak

3 tbsp dark soy sauce

1 tbsp tomato ketchup

2 garlic cloves, crushed

1 tbsp fresh lemon juice

1 tsp ground coriander

2 tbsp vegetable oil

175 g/6 oz mangetout

200 g/7 oz canned bamboo shoots,
    drained and rinsed

1 tsp sesame oil

1 Thinly slice the meat and place in a non-metallic dish together with the dark soy sauce, tomato ketchup, garlic, lemon juice and ground coriander. Mix well so that all of the meat is well coated in the marinade, cover with clingfilm and leave for at least 1 hour.

2 Heat the vegetable oil in a preheated wok. Add the meat to the wok and stir-fry for 2–4 minutes (depending on how well cooked you like your meat), until cooked through.

3 Add the mangetout and bamboo shoots to the mixture in the wok and stir-fry over a high heat, tossing frequently, for a further 5 minutes.

4 Drizzle with the sesame oil and toss well to combine. Transfer to serving dishes and serve hot.

chilli beef stir-fry salad

serves four

450 g/1 lb rump steak

2 garlic cloves, crushed

1 tsp chilli powder

½ tsp salt

1 tsp ground coriander

1 ripe avocado

2 tbsp sunflower oil

425 g/15 oz canned red kidney
    beans, drained

175 g/6 oz cherry tomatoes, halved

1 large packet tortilla chips

shredded iceberg lettuce

chopped fresh coriander, to serve

1 Using a sharp knife, slice the beef into thin strips.

2 Place the garlic, chilli powder, salt and ground coriander in a large bowl and mix until well mixed.

3 Add the strips of beef to the marinade and toss thoroughly to coat all over.

4 Using a sharp knife, peel the avocado. Slice the avocado lengthways in half and remove and discard the stone, then slice crossways to form small dice.

5 Heat the oil in a large preheated wok. Add the beef and stir-fry for 5 minutes, tossing frequently.

6 Add the kidney beans, tomatoes and avocado and heat through for 2 minutes.

7 Arrange the tortilla chips and iceberg lettuce around the edge of a serving plate and spoon the beef into the centre. Alternatively, serve the tortilla chips and lettuce separately.

8 Garnish with chopped fresh coriander and serve immediately.

beef & beans

serves four

450 g/1 lb rump or fillet steak, cut
　　into 2.5-cm/1-inch pieces

MARINADE

2 tsp cornflour

2 tbsp dark soy sauce

2 tsp peanut oil

SAUCE

2 tbsp vegetable oil

3 cloves garlic, crushed

1 small onion, cut into 8 pieces

225 g/8 oz green beans, halved

25 g/1 oz unsalted cashews

25 g/1 oz canned bamboo shoots,
　　drained and rinsed

2 tsp dark soy sauce

2 tsp Chinese rice wine or dry sherry

125 ml/4 fl oz beef stock

2 tsp cornflour

4 tsp water

salt and pepper

1 To make the marinade, mix together the cornflour, soy sauce and peanut oil.

2 Place the steak in a shallow glass bowl. Pour the marinade over the steak, turn to coat thoroughly, cover and leave to marinate in the refrigerator for at least 30 minutes.

3 To make the sauce, heat the oil in a preheated wok. Add the garlic, onion, beans, cashews and bamboo shoots and stir-fry for 2–3 minutes.

4 Remove the steak from the marinade, drain, add to the wok and stir-fry for 3–4 minutes.

5 Mix the soy sauce, Chinese rice wine or sherry and beef stock together. Blend the cornflour with the water and add to the soy sauce mixture, stir until well blended.

6 Stir the mixture into the wok and bring the sauce to the boil, stirring until thickened. Reduce the heat and leave to simmer for 2–3 minutes. Season to taste and then serve immediately.

beef & vegetables with sherry & soy sauce

serves four

2 tbsp sunflower oil

350 g/12 oz beef fillet, sliced

1 red onion, sliced

175 g/6 oz courgettes

175 g/6 oz carrots, sliced thinly

1 red pepper, deseeded and sliced

1 small head Chinese
    leaves, shredded

150 g/5½ oz beansprouts

225 g/8 oz canned bamboo shoots,
    drained and rinsed

150 g/5½ oz cashew nuts, toasted

SAUCE

3 tbsp medium sherry

3 tbsp light soy sauce

1 tsp ground ginger

1 garlic clove, crushed

1 tsp cornflour

1 tbsp tomato purée

1 Heat the sunflower oil in a large preheated wok. Add the sliced beef and red onion to the wok and stir-fry for about 4–5 minutes, or until the onion begins to soften and the meat is just browning.

2 Trim the courgettes and cut into thin, diagonal slices.

3 Add the carrots, pepper, and courgettes to the wok and stir-fry for 5 minutes.

4 Toss in the shredded Chinese leaves, beansprouts and bamboo shoots and heat through for about 2–3 minutes, or until the leaves are just beginning to wilt.

5 Scatter the cashews over the stir-fry and toss well to mix.

6 To make the sauce, mix together the sherry, soy sauce, ground ginger, garlic, cornflour and tomato purée until well mixed.

7 Pour the sauce over the stir-fry and toss to mix. Allow the sauce to bubble for 2–3 minutes, or until the juices thicken.

8 Transfer to warm serving dishes and serve at once.

beef & peppers with lemon grass

serves four

500 g/1 lb 2 oz beef fillet

2 tbsp vegetable oil

1 garlic clove, chopped finely

1 lemon grass stalk, shredded finely

2 tsp finely chopped fresh
 root ginger

1 red pepper, deseeded and
 thickly sliced

1 green pepper, deseeded and
 thickly sliced

1 onion, sliced thickly

2 tbsp lime juice

salt and pepper

cooked noodles or rice, to serve

1 If you have time, place the beef in the freezer for 30 minutes beforehand. This helps firm it up, which makes it easier to slice very thinly. Cut the beef into long, thin strips, cutting across the grain.

2 Heat the oil in a preheated wok or large, heavy-based frying pan over a high heat. Add the garlic and stir-fry for 1 minute.

3 Add the beef and stir-fry for a further 2–3 minutes, until lightly coloured. Stir in the lemon grass and ginger and remove the wok or pan from the heat.

4 Remove the beef from the wok or pan with a slotted spoon and keep warm. Add the peppers and onion to the wok or pan and stir-fry over a high heat for 2–3 minutes, until the onion is just turning golden brown and slightly softened.

5 Return the beef to the wok or pan, stir in the lime juice and season to taste with salt and pepper. Serve immediately with noodles or rice.

garlic beef with sesame seeds & soy sauce

serves four

2 tbsp sesame seeds

450 g/1 lb beef fillet

2 tbsp vegetable oil

1 green pepper, deseeded and
thinly sliced

4 garlic cloves, crushed

2 tbsp dry sherry

4 tbsp dark soy sauce

6 spring onions, sliced

cooked noodles, to serve

COOK'S TIP

You can spread the sesame
seeds out on a baking tray and
toast them under a preheated
grill until browned all over,
if you prefer.

1 Preheat a large wok or large, heavy-based frying pan until it is very hot.

2 Add the sesame seeds to the wok or frying pan and dry-fry, stirring, for 1–2 minutes, or until they just begin to brown and give off their aroma. Remove the sesame seeds from the wok and reserve until required.

3 Using a sharp knife or meat cleaver, thinly slice the beef.

4 Heat the vegetable oil in the wok or frying pan. Add the beef and stir-fry for 2–3 minutes, or until sealed on all sides.

5 Add the sliced pepper and crushed garlic and continue stir-frying for 2 minutes.

6 Add the dry sherry and soy sauce together with the spring onions. Allow the mixture in the wok or frying pan to bubble, stirring occasionally, for about 1 minute, but do not let it burn.

7 Transfer the garlic beef stir-fry to warm serving bowls and scatter with the dry-fried sesame seeds. Serve hot with noodles.

stir-fried beef with beansprouts

serves four

bunch spring onions, thinly
　　sliced lengthways

2 tbsp sunflower oil

1 garlic clove, crushed

1 tsp finely chopped fresh
　　root ginger

500 g/1 lb 2 oz beef fillet, cut into
　　thin strips

1 large red pepper, deseeded
　　and sliced

1 small fresh red chilli, deseeded
　　and chopped

350 g/12 oz beansprouts

1 small lemon grass stalk,
　　chopped finely

2 tbsp smooth peanut butter

4 tbsp coconut milk

1 tbsp rice vinegar

1 tbsp soy sauce

1 tsp soft light brown sugar

250 g/9 oz medium egg noodles

salt and pepper

1 Reserve some of the sliced spring
onions for the garnish. Heat the
sunflower oil in a preheated wok or
frying pan over a high heat. Add the
remaining spring onions, the garlic and
ginger and stir-fry for 2–3 minutes,

until softened. Add the strips of beef
and stir-fry for 4–5 minutes, until
browned all over.

2 Add the red pepper and stir-fry
for a further 3–4 minutes. Add
the chilli and beansprouts and stir-fry
for 2 minutes. Mix the lemon grass,
peanut butter, coconut milk, vinegar,
soy sauce and sugar, then
stir the mixture into the wok.

3 Meanwhile, cook the egg noodles
in lightly salted boiling water for
4 minutes, or according to the packet
instructions. Drain and stir into the wok
or frying pan, tossing to mix evenly.

4 Season to taste with salt and
pepper. Sprinkle the reserved
spring onion slices over the beef stir-fry
and serve immediately.

stir-fried beef with baby onions

serves four

450 g/1 lb beef fillet

2 tbsp light soy sauce

1 tsp chilli oil

1 tbsp tamarind paste

2 tbsp palm sugar or
   demerara sugar

2 garlic cloves, crushed

2 tbsp sunflower oil

225 g/8 oz baby onions

2 tbsp chopped fresh coriander

1 Using a sharp knife, thinly slice the beef.

2 Place the slices of beef in a large, shallow non-metallic dish.

3 Mix together the soy sauce, chilli oil, tamarind paste, palm or demerara sugar and garlic.

4 Spoon the sugar mixture over the beef. Toss well to coat the beef in the mixture, cover with clingfilm and leave to marinate for at least 1 hour.

5 Heat the sunflower oil in a pre-heated wok or large frying pan.

6 Peel the onions and cut them in half. Add the onions to the wok or pan and stir-fry for 2–3 minutes, or until just browning.

7 Add the beef and marinade juices to the wok or pan and stir-fry over a high heat for about 5 minutes.

8 Scatter with chopped fresh coriander and serve at once.

red-hot beef with cashews

serves four

500 g/1 lb 2 oz boneless, lean beef
   sirloin, sliced thinly

1 tsp vegetable oil

1 tsp sesame oil

4 tbsp unsalted cashew nuts

1 spring onion, thickly
   sliced diagonally

cucumber slices, to garnish

MARINADE

1 tbsp sesame seeds

1 garlic clove, chopped

1 tbsp finely chopped fresh
   root ginger

1 fresh red bird-eye chilli, chopped

2 tbsp dark soy sauce

1 tsp Thai red curry paste

freshly cooked rice, to serve

1 Cut the beef into 1-cm/½-inch wide strips. Place them in a large, non-metallic bowl.

2 To make the marinade, dry-fry the sesame seeds in a wok or heavy-based pan over a medium heat for 2–3 minutes.

3 Place the seeds in a mortar with the garlic, ginger and chilli and grind to a smooth paste with a pestle. Add the soy sauce and curry paste and mix well.

4 Spoon the paste over the beef strips and toss well to coat the meat evenly. Cover and leave to marinate in the refrigerator for 2–3 hours or overnight.

5 Heat a wok or heavy-based frying pan until very hot and brush with the vegetable oil. Add the beef strips and cook quickly, turning frequently, until lightly browned. Remove from the heat and spoon into a pile on a warmed serving dish.

6 Heat the sesame oil in a small pan and fry the cashew nuts until golden. Add the sliced spring onion and stir-fry for 30 seconds. Sprinkle the mixture on to the beef and serve garnished with cucumber.

pork balls with mint sauce

serves four

500 g/1 lb 2 oz lean pork mince

40 g/1½ oz fine fresh
   white breadcrumbs

½ tsp ground allspice

1 garlic clove, crushed

2 tbsp chopped fresh mint

1 egg, beaten

2 tbsp sunflower oil

1 red pepper, deseeded and
   thinly sliced

250 ml/9 fl oz chicken stock

4 pickled walnuts, sliced

salt and pepper

fresh mint, to garnish

cooked rice or noodles, to serve

1 Mix the pork mince, the breadcrumbs, allspice, garlic and half the chopped mint in a mixing bowl. Season to taste with salt and pepper, then bind together with the beaten egg.

2 Shape the meat mixture into 20 walnut-size balls with your hands, dampening your hands if it is easier for shaping.

3 Heat the sunflower oil in a preheated wok or frying pan, swirling the oil around until really hot, then stir-fry the pork balls for about 4–5 minutes, or until browned all over.

4 Remove the pork balls from the wok or frying pan with a slotted spoon as they are ready and drain thoroughly on absorbent kitchen paper.

5 Pour off all but 1 tablespoon of fat and oil from the wok or frying pan, then add the red pepper slices and stir-fry for 2–3 minutes, or until they begin to soften, but not colour.

6 Add the chicken stock and bring to the boil. Season well with salt and pepper and return the pork balls to the wok or pan, stirring well to coat in the sauce. Simmer for 7–10 minutes, turning the pork balls from time to time.

7 Add the remaining chopped mint and the pickled walnuts and continue to simmer for 2–3 minutes, turning the pork balls regularly to coat them in the sauce.

8 Adjust the seasoning and serve the pork balls immediately with rice or Chinese noodles and garnished with sprigs of fresh mint.

sweet & sour pork

serves four

450 g/1 lb pork fillet

2 tbsp sunflower oil

225 g/8 oz courgettes

1 red onion, cut into matchsticks

2 garlic cloves, crushed

225 g/8 oz carrots, cut into
   thin sticks

1 red pepper, deseeded and sliced

100 g/3½ oz baby corn cobs

100 g/3½ oz button
   mushrooms, halved

175 g/6 oz fresh pineapple, cubed

100 g/3½ oz beansprouts

150 ml/5 fl oz pineapple juice

1 tbsp cornflour

2 tbsp soy sauce

3 tbsp tomato ketchup

1 tbsp white wine vinegar

1 tbsp clear honey

COOK'S TIP

If you prefer a crisper
coating, toss the pork in a
mixture of cornflour and
egg white and deep-fry in
the wok in step 2.

1 Using a sharp knife, thinly slice the pork fillet into even-size pieces.

2 Heat the sunflower oil in a large preheated wok. Add the pork to the wok and stir-fry for 10 minutes, or until the pork is completely cooked through and beginning to turn crispy at the edges.

3 Meanwhile, cut the courgettes into thin sticks.

4 Add the onion, garlic, carrots, courgettes, red pepper, corn cobs and mushrooms to the wok and stir-fry for a further 5 minutes.

5 Add the pineapple cubes and beansprouts to the wok and stir-fry for 2 minutes.

6 Mix together the pineapple juice, cornflour, soy sauce, tomato ketchup, white wine vinegar and honey.

7 Pour the sweet-and-sour mixture into the wok and cook over a high heat, tossing frequently, until the juices thicken. Transfer the sweet-and-sour pork to serving bowls and serve hot.

pork fillet with crunchy satay sauce

serves four

150 g/5½ oz carrots

2 tbsp sunflower oil

350 g/12 oz pork fillet,
     sliced thinly

1 onion, sliced

2 garlic cloves, crushed

1 yellow pepper, deseeded
     and sliced

150 g/5½ oz mangetout

75 g/2¾ oz fine asparagus

chopped salted peanuts, to serve

SATAY SAUCE

6 tbsp crunchy peanut butter

6 tbsp coconut milk

1 tsp chilli flakes

1 garlic clove, crushed

1 tsp tomato purée

1 Using a sharp knife, slice the carrots into thin sticks.

2 Heat the oil in a large, preheated wok. Add the pork, onion and garlic and stir-fry for 5 minutes, or until the pork is cooked through.

3 Add the carrots, yellow pepper, mangetout and asparagus to the wok and stir-fry for 5 minutes.

4 To make the satay sauce, place the peanut butter, coconut milk, chilli flakes, garlic and tomato purée in a small pan and heat gently, stirring, until well mixed. Be careful not to let the sauce stick to the base of the pan.

5 Transfer the stir-fry to warm serving plates. Spoon the satay sauce over the stir-fry and scatter with chopped peanuts. Serve immediately.

stir-fried pork with pasta & vegetables

serves four

3 tbsp sunflower oil

350 g/12 oz pork fillet, cut into
   thin strips

450 g/1 lb dried taglioni

8 shallots, sliced

2 garlic cloves, chopped finely

2.5-cm/1-inch piece of fresh root
   ginger, grated

1 fresh green chilli, chopped finely

1 red pepper, deseeded and
   thinly sliced

1 green pepper, deseeded and
   thinly sliced

3 courgettes, sliced thinly

2 tbsp ground almonds

1 tsp ground cinnamon

1 tbsp oyster sauce

55 g/2 oz creamed coconut, grated

salt and pepper

1 Heat the sunflower oil in a preheated wok. Season the pork with salt and pepper to taste, add to the wok and stir-fry for 5 minutes.

2 Meanwhile, bring a large pan of lightly salted water to the boil. Add the taglioni, bring back to the boil and cook for about 10 minutes, until just tender, but still firm to the bite – al dente. Drain the pasta thoroughly and keep warm.

3 Add the shallots, garlic, ginger and chilli to the wok and stir-fry for 2 minutes. Add the peppers and courgettes and stir-fry for 1 minute.

4 Finally, add the ground almonds, ground cinnamon, oyster sauce and creamed coconut to the wok and stir-fry for about 1 minute.

5 Transfer the taglioni to a warmed serving dish. Top with the stir-fry and serve immediately.

five-spice crispy pork with egg-fried rice

serves four

275 g/9½ oz long-grain
   white rice

600 ml/1 pint cold water

350 g/12 oz pork fillet

2 tsp Chinese five-spice powder

4 tbsp cornflour

3 large eggs

25 g/1 oz demerara sugar

2 tbsp sunflower oil

1 onion

2 garlic cloves, crushed

100 g/3½ oz carrots, diced

1 red pepper, deseeded and diced

100 g/3½ oz peas

2 tbsp butter

salt and pepper

1 Rinse the rice under cold running water. Place the rice in a large saucepan, add the cold water and a pinch of salt. Bring to the boil, cover, then reduce the heat and simmer for about 9 minutes, or until all of the liquid has been absorbed and the rice is tender.

2 Meanwhile, slice the pork fillet into very thin, even-size pieces, using a sharp knife or meat cleaver. Reserve the pork strips until required.

3 Stir together the Chinese five-spice powder, cornflour, 1 egg and the demerara sugar. Toss the pork in the mixture until coated.

4 Heat the sunflower oil in a preheated wok or frying pan. Add the pork and cook over a high heat until the pork is cooked through and crispy. Remove the pork from the wok with a slotted spoon and keep warm.

5 Using a sharp knife, cut the onion into dice.

6 Add the onion, garlic, carrots, red pepper and peas to the wok and stir-fry for 5 minutes.

7 Return the pork to the wok together with the cooked rice and stir-fry for 5 minutes.

8 Heat the butter in a frying pan. Beat the remaining eggs, add to the pan and cook until set. Turn out on to a clean board and slice thinly. Toss the strips of egg into the rice mixture and serve immediately.

pork with mooli

serves four

4 tbsp vegetable oil

450 g/1 lb pork fillet

1 aubergine

225 g/8 oz mooli

2 garlic cloves, crushed

3 tbsp light soy sauce

2 tbsp sweet chilli sauce

cooked rice or noodles, to serve

COOK'S TIP

Mooli are long white vegetables common in Chinese cooking. Usually grated, they have a milder flavour than red radish. They are generally available in most large supermarkets.

1 Heat 2 tablespoons of the vegetable oil in a large preheated wok or frying pan.

2 Using a sharp knife, thinly slice the pork into even-size pieces.

3 Add the slices of pork to the wok or frying pan and stir-fry for about 5 minutes.

4 Using a sharp knife, trim and dice the aubergine. Peel and thinly slice the mooli.

5 Add the remaining vegetable oil to the wok.

6 Add the diced aubergine to the wok or frying pan together with the garlic and stir-fry for 5 minutes.

7 Add the mooli to the wok and stir-fry for about 2 minutes.

8 Stir the soy sauce and sweet chilli sauce into the mixture in the wok and cook until heated through.

9 Transfer the pork to serving bowls and serve with rice or noodles.

twice-cooked pork with peppers

serves four

15 g/½ oz Chinese
   dried mushrooms

450g/1 lb pork leg steaks

2 tbsp vegetable oil

1 onion, sliced

1 red pepper, deseeded and diced

1 green pepper, deseeded and diced

1 yellow pepper, deseeded
   and diced

4 tbsp oyster sauce

VARIATION

Use open-cap mushrooms,
sliced, instead of Chinese
mushrooms, if you prefer.

---

1 Place the mushrooms in a large bowl. Pour over enough boiling water to cover and leave to stand for 20 minutes.

2 Using a sharp knife, trim any excess fat from the pork steaks. Cut the pork into thin strips.

3 Bring a large saucepan of water to the boil. Add the pork to the boiling water and cook for 5 minutes.

4 Remove the pork from the pan with a slotted spoon and leave to drain thoroughly.

5 Heat the oil in a large preheated wok. Add the pork to the wok and stir-fry for about 5 minutes.

6 Remove the mushrooms from the water and drain thoroughly. Roughly chop the mushrooms.

7 Add the mushrooms, onion and the peppers to the wok and stir-fry for 5 minutes.

8 Stir in the oyster sauce and cook for 2–3 minutes. Transfer to serving bowls and serve immediately.

spicy pork balls

COOK'S TIP

Add a few teaspoons of chilli
sauce to a can of chopped
tomatoes, if you can't find the
flavoured variety.

1 Place the pork mince in a large mixing bowl. Add the shallots, garlic, cumin seeds, chilli powder, breadcrumbs and beaten egg and mix together well.

2 Form the mixture into small balls between the dampened palms of your hands.

3 Heat the oil in a large preheated wok or heavy-based frying pan. Add the pork balls and stir-fry, in batches, over a high heat for about 5 minutes, or until sealed on all sides.

4 Add the tomatoes, soy sauce and water chestnuts and bring to the boil. Return the pork balls to the wok, reduce the heat and simmer gently for 15 minutes.

5 Scatter with chopped fresh coriander and serve hot.

pork with plums

serves four

450 g/1 lb pork fillet

1 tbsp cornflour

2 tbsp light soy sauce

2 tbsp Chinese rice wine

4 tsp light brown sugar

pinch of ground cinnamon

5 tsp vegetable oil

2 garlic cloves, crushed

2 spring onions, chopped

4 tbsp plum sauce

1 tbsp hoisin sauce

150 ml/5 fl oz water

dash of chilli sauce

TO GARNISH

fried plum quarters

spring onions

1 Cut the pork fillet into thin slices.

2 Mix the cornflour, soy sauce, rice wine, sugar and ground cinnamon in a small bowl.

3 Place the pork in a shallow dish and pour the cornflour mixture over it. Toss the meat in the marinade until it is completely coated. Cover and leave to marinate for 30 minutes.

4 Remove the pork from the dish, reserving the marinade.

5 Heat the oil in a preheated wok or large frying pan. Add the pork and stir-fry for 3–4 minutes, until a light golden colour.

6 Stir in the garlic, spring onions, plum sauce, hoisin sauce, water and chilli sauce. Bring the sauce to the boil. Reduce the heat, cover and leave to simmer for 8–10 minutes, or until the pork is cooked through and tender.

7 Stir in the reserved marinade and cook, stirring, for about 5 minutes.

8 Transfer the pork stir-fry to a warm serving dish and garnish with fried plum quarters and spring onions. Serve immediately.

garlic-infused lamb with soy sauce

serves four

450 g/1 lb lamb loin fillet

2 garlic cloves

2 tbsp groundnut oil

3 tbsp dry sherry or Chinese rice wine

3 tbsp dark soy sauce

1 tsp cornflour

2 tbsp water

2 tbsp butter

1 Using a sharp knife, make small slits in the flesh of the lamb.

2 Carefully peel the garlic cloves and cut them into slices, using a sharp knife.

3 Push the slices of garlic into the slits in the lamb. Place the garlic-infused lamb in a shallow dish.

4 In a small bowl, mix together 1 tablespoon each of the groundnut oil, dry sherry or rice wine and dark soy sauce. Drizzle this mixture over the lamb and turn to coat thoroughly. Cover with clingfilm and leave to marinate for at least 1 hour, preferably overnight.

5 Drain the lamb, reserving the marinade. Using a sharp knife or meat cleaver, thinly slice the meat.

6 Heat the remaining oil in a preheated wok or large frying pan. Add the marinated lamb and stir-fry for 5 minutes.

7 Add the marinade juices and the remaining sherry and soy sauce to the wok or frying pan and allow the juices to bubble for 5 minutes.

8 Blend the cornflour to a smooth paste with the water. Add the cornflour mixture to the wok or pan and cook, stirring occasionally, until the juices start to thicken.

9 Cut the butter into small pieces. Add the butter to the wok or frying pan and stir until the butter melts. Transfer the lamb to serving dishes and serve immediately.

thai-style lamb with lime leaves

serves four

2 fresh red chillies

2 tbsp groundnut oil

2 garlic cloves, crushed

4 shallots, chopped

2 lemon grass stalks, sliced

6 kaffir lime leaves

1 tbsp tamarind paste

25 g/1 oz palm sugar

450 g/1 lb lean lamb (leg or
  loin fillet)

600 ml/1 pint coconut milk

175 g/6 oz cherry tomatoes, halved

1 tbsp chopped fresh coriander

freshly cooked fragrant rice, to serve

COOK'S TIP

When buying fresh coriander,
look for bright green, unwilted
leaves. To store it, wash and
dry the leaves, leaving them
on the stem. Wrap the leaves
in damp kitchen paper and
keep them in a plastic bag
in the refrigerator.

1 Using a sharp knife, deseed and
very finely chop the red chillies.

2 Heat the oil in a large preheated
wok or frying pan.

3 Add the garlic, shallots, lemon
grass, lime leaves, tamarind
paste, palm sugar and chillies and stir-
fry for about 2 minutes.

4 Using a sharp knife, cut the lamb
into thin strips or cubes. Add the
lamb to the wok or frying pan and
stir-fry for about 5 minutes, tossing
well so that the lamb is evenly coated
in the spice mixture.

5 Pour the coconut milk into the
wok or pan and bring to the boil.
Reduce the heat and simmer gently
for 20 minutes.

6 Add the tomatoes and coriander
and simmer, stirring occasionally,
for a further 5 minutes. Transfer to
serving plates and serve hot with
freshly cooked fragrant rice.

lamb with black bean sauce & peppers

serves four

450 g/1 lb lamb neck fillet or
    boneless leg of lamb chops
1 egg white, beaten lightly
4 tbsp cornflour
1 tsp Chinese five-spice powder
3 tbsp sunflower oil
1 red onion
1 red pepper, deseeded and sliced
1 green pepper, deseeded
    and sliced
1 yellow or orange pepper,
    deseeded and sliced
5 tbsp black bean sauce
cooked rice or noodles, to serve

1 Using a sharp knife, slice the lamb into very thin strips.

2 Mix together the egg white, cornflour and Chinese five-spice powder. Toss the lamb strips in the mixture until evenly coated.

3 Heat the oil in a preheated wok and stir-fry the lamb over a high heat for 5 minutes, or until it crispens around the edges.

4 Slice the red onion. Add the onion and pepper slices to the wok and stir-fry for 5–6 minutes, or until the vegetables just begin to soften.

5 Stir the black bean sauce into the mixture in the wok and gently heat through.

6 Transfer the lamb and sauce to warm serving plates and serve immediately with freshly cooked rice or noodles.

spring onions & lamb with oyster sauce

serves four

450 g/1 lb lamb leg steaks

1 tsp ground Sezchuan peppercorns

1 tbsp groundnut oil

2 garlic cloves

8 spring onions, sliced

2 tbsp dark soy sauce

175 g/6 oz Chinese leaves

6 tbsp oyster sauce

prawn crackers, to serve (optional)

COOK'S TIP

Oyster sauce is made from oysters which are cooked in brine and soy sauce. Sold in bottles, it will keep in the refrigerator for months.

1 Using a sharp knife, remove any excess fat from the lamb. Slice the lamb thinly.

2 Sprinkle the ground Sezchuan peppercorns over the meat and toss together until well mixed.

3 Heat the groundnut oil in a preheated wok or large heavy-based frying pan.

4 Add the lamb to the wok or frying pan and stir-fry for 5 minutes.

5 Meanwhile, crush the garlic with a pestle and mortar and slice the spring onions. Add the garlic, spring onions and soy sauce to the wok and stir-fry for 2 minutes.

6 Coarsely shred the Chinese leaves and add them to the wok together with the oyster sauce. Stir-fry for a further 2 minutes, or until the Chinese leaves have just wilted and the cooking juices are bubbling.

7 Transfer the lamb stir-fry to individual warm serving bowls and serve immediately with prawn crackers (if using).

lamb with satay sauce

serves four

450 g/1 lb lamb loin fillet

1 tbsp mild curry paste

150 ml/5 fl oz coconut milk

2 garlic cloves, crushed

½ tsp chilli powder

½ tsp ground cumin

SATAY SAUCE

1 tbsp corn oil

1 onion, diced

6 tbsp crunchy peanut butter

1 tsp tomato purée

1 tsp fresh lime juice

100 ml/3½ fl oz water

COOK'S TIP

Soak the wooden skewers in
cold water for 30 minutes before
grilling to prevent the skewers
from burning.

1 Using a sharp knife, thinly slice the lamb and place in a large dish.

2 Mix together the curry paste, coconut milk, garlic, chilli powder and cumin in a bowl. Pour over the lamb, toss well, cover and marinate for 30 minutes.

3 To make the satay sauce. Heat the oil in a large wok and stir-fry the onion for 5 minutes, then reduce the heat and cook for 5 minutes.

4 Stir in the peanut butter, tomato purée, lime juice and water.

5 Thread the lamb on to wooden skewers, reserving the marinade.

6 Grill the lamb skewers under a hot grill for 6–8 minutes, turning once.

7 Add the reserved marinade to the wok, bring to the boil and cook for 5 minutes. Serve the lamb skewers with the satay sauce.

stir-fried lamb with orange

serves four

450 g/1 lb lamb mince

2 garlic cloves, crushed

1 tsp cumin seeds

1 tsp ground coriander

1 red onion, sliced

finely grated rind and juice of
   1 orange

2 tbsp light soy sauce

1 orange, peeled and segmented

salt and pepper

snipped fresh chives, to garnish

1 Heat a wok or large, heavy-based frying pan, without adding any cooking oil.

2 Add the lamb mince to the wok or pan. Dry-fry the lamb for 5 minutes, or until the meat is evenly browned. Drain away any excess fat from the wok or pan.

3 Add the garlic, cumin seeds, ground coriander and red onion to the wok or pan and stir-fry for a further 5 minutes.

4 Stir in the finely grated orange rind and juice and the soy sauce,

mixing until thoroughly mixed. Cover, reduce the heat and simmer gently, stirring occasionally, for 15 minutes.

5 Remove the lid, increase the heat and add the orange segments. Stir to mix.

6 Season to taste with salt and pepper and heat through for a further 2–3 minutes, stirring and tossing constantly.

7 Transfer the lamb stir-fry to individual warm serving plates and garnish with snipped fresh chives. Serve immediately.

110

lamb's liver with green peppers & sherry

serves four

450 g/1 lb lamb's liver

3 tbsp cornflour

2 tbsp groundnut oil

1 onion, sliced

2 garlic cloves, crushed

2 green peppers, deseeded
and sliced

2 tbsp tomato purée

3 tbsp dry sherry

2 tbsp dark soy sauce

1 Using a sharp knife, trim any excess fat from the lamb's liver. Slice the lamb's liver into thin strips.

2 Place 2 tablespoons of the cornflour in a bowl.

3 Add the strips of lamb's liver to the cornflour and toss well until coated evenly all over.

4 Heat the groundnut oil in a large preheated wok.

5 Add the lamb's liver, onion, garlic and green pepper to the wok and stir-fry for 6–7 minutes, or until the lamb's liver is just cooked through and the vegetables are tender.

6 Mix together the tomato purée, dry sherry, the remaining cornflour and the soy sauce. Stir the mixture into the wok and cook, stirring constantly, for a further 2 minutes, or until the juices have thickened. Transfer to individual warm serving bowls and serve immediately.

sweet & sour venison stir-fry

serves four

bunch of spring onions

1 red pepper

100 g/3½ oz mangetout

100 g/3½ oz baby corn cobs

350 g/12 oz lean venison steak

1 tbsp vegetable oil

1 garlic clove, crushed

2.5-cm/1-inch piece fresh root
ginger, chopped finely

3 tbsp light soy sauce, plus extra
for serving

1 tbsp white wine vinegar

2 tbsp dry sherry

2 tsp clear honey

225 g/8 oz can pineapple pieces in
natural juice, drained

25 g/1 oz beansprouts

cooked rice, to serve

1 Cut the spring onions into 2.5-cm
/1-inch pieces. Halve and deseed
the red pepper and cut it into 2.5 -cm/
1-inch pieces. Trim the mangetout and
baby corn cobs.

2 Trim any fat from the meat and
cut it into thin strips. Heat the oil
in a preheated wok or large frying pan
until hot and stir-fry the meat, garlic
and ginger for 5 minutes.

3 Add the spring onions, red
pepper, mangetout and baby corn
cobs, then stir in the soy sauce,
vinegar, sherry and honey. Stir-fry for
a further 5 minutes.

4 Carefully stir in the pineapple
pieces and beansprouts and
cook for a further 1–2 minutes to heat
through. Serve with freshly cooked rice
and extra soy sauce for dipping.

VARIATION

For a nutritious meal-in-one,
cook 225 g/8 oz egg noodles in
boiling water for 3–4 minutes.
Drain and add to the pan in
step 4, with the pineapple and
beansprouts. Add an extra
2 tablespoons soy sauce with
the pineapple and beansprouts.

Fish & Seafood

Throughout the Far Eastern countries, fish and seafood play a major role in the diet of the inhabitants; this is because these foods are both plentiful and very healthy. They are also very versatile: there are many different ways of cooking fish and seafood in a wok – they may be steamed, deep-fried or stir-fried with a range of delicious spices and sauces.

Japan is famed for its sushimi, or raw fish, but this is just one of the wide range of fish dishes served. Fish and seafood are offered at every meal in Japan, many of them cooked in a wok.

When buying fish and seafood for the recipes in this chapter, freshness is imperative to flavour, so be sure to buy and use the fish that you have chosen as soon as possible, preferably on the same day.

tuna & vegetable stir-fry

serves four

225 g/8 oz carrots

1 onion

175 g/6 oz baby corn cobs

2 tbsp corn oil

175 g/6 oz mangetout

450 g/1 lb fresh tuna

2 tbsp Thai fish sauce

1 tbsp palm sugar

finely grated rind and juice of
   1 orange

2 tbsp sherry

1 tsp cornflour

cooked rice or noodles, to serve

VARIATION

Try using swordfish steaks
instead of the tuna. Swordfish
steaks are now widely
available and are similar in
texture to tuna.

---

1 Using a sharp knife, cut the carrots into thin sticks, slice the onion and halve the baby corn cobs.

2 Heat the corn oil in a large preheated wok or frying pan.

3 Add the onion, carrots, mangetout and baby corn cobs to the wok or frying pan and stir-fry for 5 minutes.

4 Using a sharp knife, thinly slice the fresh tuna. (This is easier if it has been chilled in the freezer.)

5 Add the tuna slices to the wok or frying pan and stir-fry for about 2–3 minutes, or until the tuna turns opaque.

6 Mix together the fish sauce, palm sugar, orange rind and juice, sherry and cornflour. in a bowl.

7 Pour the mixture over the tuna and vegetables and cook for 2 minutes, or until the juices thicken. Serve the stir-fry with rice or noodles.

stir-fried ginger monkfish

serves four

450 g/1 lb monkfish tail

1 tbsp grated fresh root ginger

2 tbsp sweet chilli sauce

1 tbsp corn oil

100 g/3½ oz fine asparagus

3 spring onions, sliced

1 tsp sesame oil

1 Carefully remove all the grey membrane covering the monkfish.Using a sharp knife, cut along the monkfish tail on either side of the central bone. Remove and discard the bone. Slice the flesh into thin, flat rounds. Reserve.

2 Mix together the grated root ginger and sweet chilli sauce in a small bowl until thoroughly blended. Brush the ginger and chilli sauce mixture over the monkfish pieces, using a pastry brush.

3 Heat the corn oil in a large preheated wok or heavy-based frying pan.

4 Add the monkfish pieces, asparagus and spring onions to the wok or frying pan and stir-fry for about 5 minutes. Stir the mixture gently so that the fish pieces do not break up.

5 Remove the wok or frying pan from the heat, drizzle the sesame oil over the stir-fry and toss gently until well mixed.

6 Transfer the stir-fried gingered monkfish to warm serving plates and serve immediately.

monkfish & okra balti

serves four

750 g/1 lb 10 oz monkfish fillet, cut
    into 3-cm/1¼-inch cubes

250 g/9 oz okra

2 tbsp sunflower oil

1 onion, sliced

1 garlic clove, crushed

2.5-cm/1-inch piece fresh root
    ginger, sliced

150 ml/5 fl oz coconut milk or
    fish stock

2 tsp garam masala

MARINADE

3 tbsp lemon juice

grated rind of 1 lemon

¼ tsp aniseed

½ tsp salt

½ tsp pepper

TO GARNISH

4 lime wedges

fresh coriander sprigs

1 To make the marinade, mix the ingredients together in a bowl. Stir the monkfish into the bowl and leave to marinate for 1 hour.

2 Bring a saucepan of water to the boil, add the okra and boil for 4–5 minutes. Drain and cut into 1-cm/½-inch slices.

3 Heat the oil in a preheated wok, add the onion and stir-fry until golden brown. Add the garlic and ginger and fry for 1 minute. Add the fish with the marinade and stir-fry for 2 minutes.

4 Stir in the okra, coconut milk or fish stock and the garam masala and simmer for 10 minutes. Serve garnished with lime wedges and fresh coriander.

fried fish with coconut & basil

serves four

2 tbsp vegetable oil

450 g/1 lb cod fillet, skinned

25 g/1 oz seasoned flour

1 garlic clove, crushed

2 tbsp Thai red curry paste

1 tbsp Thai fish sauce

300 ml/10 fl oz coconut milk

175 g/6 oz cherry tomatoes, halved

20 fresh basil leaves

freshly cooked fragrant rice, to serve

COOK'S TIP

Take care not to overcook the
dish once the tomatoes are
added, otherwise they will
break down and the skins
will come away.

1 Heat the vegetable oil in a large preheated wok.

2 Using a sharp knife, cut the fish into large cubes, removing any bones with a pair of clean tweezers.

3 Place the seasoned flour in a bowl. Add the cubes of fish and mix until well coated.

4 Add the coated fish to the wok and stir-fry over a high heat for 3–4 minutes, or until the fish just begins to brown at the edges.

5 In a small bowl, mix together the garlic, curry paste, fish sauce and coconut milk. Pour the mixture over the fish and bring to the boil.

6 Add the tomatoes and simmer for 5 minutes.

7 Roughly chop or tear the fresh basil leaves. Add the basil to the wok, stir to mix, taking care not to break up the cubes of fish.

8 Transfer to serving plates and serve hot with freshly cooked fragrant rice.

stir-fried cod with mango

serves four

175 g/6 oz carrots

2 tbsp vegetable oil

1 red onion, sliced

1 red pepper, deseeded and sliced

1 green pepper, deseeded
and sliced

450 g/1 lb cod fillet, skinned

1 ripe mango

1 tsp cornflour

1 tbsp light soy sauce

100 ml/3½ fl oz tropical fruit juice

1 tbsp lime juice

1 tbsp chopped fresh coriander,
to garnish

1 Using a sharp knife, slice the carrots into thin sticks.

2 Heat the oil in a preheated wok and stir-fry the onion, carrots and peppers for 5 minutes.

3 Using a sharp knife, cut the cod into small cubes. Peel the mango, then carefully remove the flesh from the centre stone. Cut the flesh into thin slices.

4 Add the cod and mango to the wok and stir-fry for a further 4–5 minutes, or until the fish is cooked through. Be careful not to break up the fish.

5 Mix together the cornflour, soy sauce, fruit juice and lime juice. Pour the mixture into the wok and stir until the mixture bubbles and the juices thicken. Sprinkle with coriander and serve immediately.

braised fish fillets

serves four

3–4 small Chinese dried mushrooms

300–350 g/10½–12 oz fish fillets

1 tsp salt

½ egg white, lightly beaten

1 tsp cornflour

600 ml/1 pint vegetable oil

1 tsp finely chopped fresh
   root ginger

2 spring onions, chopped finely

1 garlic clove, chopped finely

½ small green pepper, deseeded
   and cut into small cubes

½ small carrot, sliced thinly

60 g/2 oz canned sliced bamboo
   shoots, rinsed and drained

½ tsp sugar

1 tbsp light soy sauce

1 tsp rice wine or dry sherry

1 tbsp chilli bean sauce

2–3 tbsp vegetable stock or water

a few drops of sesame oil

1 Soak the dried mushrooms in a bowl of warm water for 30 minutes. Drain thoroughly on kitchen paper, reserving the soaking water for stock or soup. Squeeze the mushrooms to extract all of the moisture, cut off and discard any hard stems and slice thinly.

2 Cut the fish into bite-size pieces, then place in a shallow dish and mix with a pinch of salt, the egg white and cornflour, turning the fish to coat well.

3 Heat the oil in a preheated wok. Add the fish pieces to the wok and deep-fry for about 1 minute. Remove the fish pieces with a slotted spoon and drain on kitchen paper.

4 Pour off the excess oil, leaving about 1 tablespoon in the wok. Add the ginger, spring onions and garlic to flavour the oil for a few seconds, then add the green pepper, carrots and bamboo shoots and stir-fry for about 1 minute.

5 Add the sugar, soy sauce, wine, chilli bean sauce, stock or water, and the remaining salt and bring to the boil. Add the fish pieces, stirring to coat with the sauce, and braise for 1 minute. Sprinkle with sesame oil and serve.

coconut prawns

COOK'S TIP

If the prawns are frozen, thaw
them thoroughly before cooking.
Raw prawns are best for this
dish, but if you cannot obtain
them, buy unpeeled cooked
prawns and peel them yourself.

1 Mix together the desiccated
coconut, white breadcrumbs,
Chinese five-spice powder, salt and
lime rind in a bowl.

2 Lightly whisk the egg white in a
separate bowl.

3 Rinse the prawns under cold
running water, and pat dry with
kitchen paper.

4 Dip the prawns into the egg
white, then into the coconut and
breadcrumb mixture, so that they are
evenly coated.

5 Heat about 5-cm/2-inches of
sunflower or corn oil in a large
preheated wok.

6 Add the prawns to the wok and
stir-fry for about 5 minutes, or
until golden and crispy.

7 Remove the prawns with a
slotted spoon and drain on
kitchen paper.

8 Transfer the coconut prawns to
warm serving dishes and garnish
with lemon wedges. Serve immediately
with soy or chilli sauce.

prawn omelette

serves four

2 tbsp sunflower oil

4 spring onions

350 g/12 oz cooked peeled prawns

100 g/3½ oz beansprouts

1 tsp cornflour

1 tbsp light soy sauce

6 eggs

3 tbsp water

1 Heat the sunflower oil in a large preheated wok or frying pan.

2 Using a sharp knife, trim the spring onions and cut into slices.

3 Add the prawns, spring onions and beansprouts to the wok or frying pan and stir-fry for 2 minutes.

4 In a small bowl, mix together the cornflour and soy sauce until well mixed.

5 In a separate bowl, beat the eggs with the water, using a fork, and then blend thoroughly with the cornflour and soy mixture.

6 Add the egg mixture to the wok or frying pan and cook for 5–6 minutes, or until the mixture sets.

7 Transfer the omelette to a warm serving plate and cut into quarters to serve.

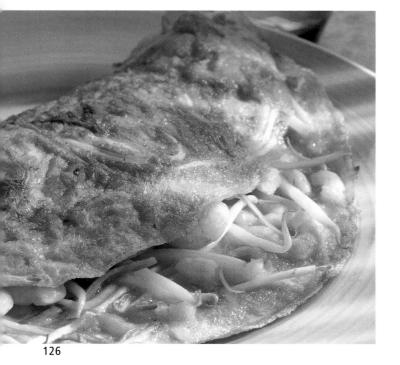

prawns with spicy tomatoes

serves four

2 tbsp corn oil

1 onion

2 garlic cloves, crushed

1 tsp cumin seeds

1 tbsp demerara sugar

400 g/14 oz canned
   chopped tomatoes

1 tbsp sun-dried tomato purée

1 tbsp chopped fresh basil

450 g/1 lb raw king prawns, peeled

salt and pepper

COOK'S TIP

Cut along the back of each
prawn with a sharp knife and
remove the dark vein with the
point of the knife.

1 Heat the corn oil in a large
preheated wok.

2 Using a sharp knife, finely chop
the onion.

3 Add the onion and garlic to the
wok and stir-fry for 2–3 minutes,
or until softened.

4 Stir in the cumin seeds and stir-fry
for 1 minute.

5 Add the sugar, chopped tomatoes
and sun-dried tomato purée to
the wok. Bring the mixture to the boil,
then reduce the heat and simmer
gently for 10 minutes.

6 Add the basil, prawns and salt
and pepper to taste to the mixture
in the wok. Increase the heat and cook
for a further 2–3 minutes, or until the
prawns are completely cooked through.
Serve immediately.

spicy thai seafood stew

serves four

200 g/7 oz prepared squid

500 g/1 lb 2 oz firm white fish fillet, preferably monkfish or halibut

1 tbsp sunflower oil

4 shallots, chopped finely

2 garlic cloves, chopped finely

2 tbsp Thai green curry paste

2 small lemon grass stalks, chopped finely

1 tsp shrimp paste

500 ml/18 fl oz coconut milk

200 g/7 oz raw tiger prawns, peeled

12 live clams, scrubbed

8 fresh basil leaves, shredded finely, plus extra to garnish

cooked rice, to serve

COOK'S TIP

If you prefer, fresh mussels in shells can be used instead of clams – add them in step 4 and follow the recipe.

1 Cut the squid body cavities into thick rings and cut the fish fillet into bite-size chunks.

2 Heat the oil in a preheated wok or large frying pan and stir-fry the shallots, garlic and curry paste for 1–2 minutes. Add the lemon grass and shrimp paste, stir in the coconut milk and bring to the boil.

3 Reduce the heat to low. When the liquid is simmering gently, add the white fish chunks, squid rings and prawns to the pan. Stir and then simmer for 2 minutes.

4 Add the clams and simmer for 1 further minute, until the clams have opened. Discard any clams that do not open.

5 Scatter the shredded basil leaves over the seafood stew and serve immediately, garnished with whole basil leaves and spooned over a bed of cooked rice.

vegetables with prawns & egg

serves four

225 g/8 oz courgettes

3 tbsp vegetable oil

2 eggs

2 tbsp water

225 g/8 oz carrots, grated

1 onion, sliced

150 g/5½ oz beansprouts

225 g/8 oz cooked peeled prawns

2 tbsp light soy sauce

pinch of Chinese five-spice powder

25 g/1 oz peanuts, chopped

2 tbsp chopped fresh coriander

1 Finely grate the courgettes by hand or in a food processor.

2 Heat 1 tablespoon of the vegetable oil in a large preheated wok.

3 Beat the eggs with the water, pour the mixture into the wok and cook for 2–3 minutes, or until the omelette sets.

4 Remove the omelette from the wok and transfer to a board. Fold the omelette, cut it into thin strips and reserve until required.

5 Add the remaining oil to the wok. Add the carrots, onion and courgettes and stir-fry for 5 minutes.

6 Add the beansprouts and prawns to the wok and cook for a further 2 minutes, or until the prawns are heated through.

7 Add the soy sauce, Chinese five-spice powder and peanuts to the wok, together with the strips of omelette and heat through. Garnish with chopped fresh coriander and serve immediately.

prawns with crispy ginger

serves four

5-cm/2-inch piece fresh root ginger

groundnut oil, for frying

1 onion, diced

225 g/8 oz carrots, diced

100 g/3½ oz frozen peas

100 g/3½ oz beansprouts

450 g/1 lb raw king prawns, peeled

1 tsp Chinese five-spice powder

1 tbsp tomato purée

1 tbsp light soy sauce

1 Using a sharp knife, peel the ginger and slice it into very thin sticks.

2 Heat about 2.5-cm/1-inch of oil in a large preheated wok. Add the ginger and stir-fry for 1 minute, or until the ginger is crispy. Remove the ginger with a slotted spoon and drain on kitchen paper.

3 Drain all of the oil from the wok except for about 2 tablespoons. Add the onions and carrots to the wok and stir-fry for 5 minutes. Add the peas and beansprouts and stir-fry for a further 2 minutes.

4 Rinse the prawns under cold running water and pat dry with kitchen paper.

5 Mix the Chinese five-spice powder, tomato purée and soy sauce in a bowl. Brush the mixture over the prawns.

6 Add the prawns to the wok and stir-fry for 2 minutes, or until the prawns are completely cooked through. Transfer the prawn mixture to warm individual serving bowls and top with the reserved crispy ginger. Serve immediately.

stir-fried crab claws with chilli

serves four

700 g/1 lb 9 oz crab claws

1 tbsp corn oil

2 garlic cloves, crushed

1 tbsp grated fresh root ginger

3 fresh red chillies, deseeded and
    finely chopped

2 tbsp sweet chilli sauce

3 tbsp tomato ketchup

300 ml/10 fl oz fish stock

1 tbsp cornflour

salt and pepper

1 tbsp snipped fresh chives,
    to garnish

COOK'S TIP

If crab claws are not easily
available, use a whole crab, cut
into 8 pieces, instead.

1 Gently crack the crab claws with a
nut cracker. This process will allow
the flavours of the chilli, garlic and
ginger to penetrate the crab meat.

2 Heat the corn oil in a large
preheated wok.

3 Add the crab claws to the wok
and stir-fry for about 5 minutes.

4 Add the garlic, ginger and
chillies to the wok and stir-fry
for 1 minute, tossing the crab claws
to coat all over.

5 Mix together the sweet chilli
sauce, tomato ketchup, fish stock
and cornflour in a small bowl. Add this
mixture to the wok and cook, stirring
occasionally, until the sauce starts to
thicken and reduce slightly.

6 Season the mixture in the wok
with salt and pepper to taste.

7 Transfer the crab claws and
chilli sauce to warm serving
dishes, garnish with snipped fresh
chives and serve.

rice with crab & mussels

serves four

300 g/10½ oz long-grain rice

175 g/6 oz white crab meat, fresh,
   canned or frozen (thawed if
   frozen), or 8 seafood sticks,
   thawed if frozen

2 tbsp sunflower oil

2.5-cm/1-inch piece fresh root
   ginger, grated

4 spring onions, sliced thinly
   diagonally

125 g/4½ oz mangetout, cut into
   2–3 pieces

½ tsp ground turmeric

1 tsp ground cumin

2 x 200 g/7 oz jars mussels, well
   drained, or 350 g/12 oz frozen
   mussels, thawed

425 g/15 oz canned beansprouts,
   well drained

salt and pepper

1 Cook the rice in a large pan of
   lightly salted, boiling water for
12–15 minutes, until tender. Drain,
rinse with freshly boiled water and
drain again.

2 Meanwhile, extract the crab meat,
   if using fresh crab. Flake the crab
meat or cut the seafood sticks into 3 or
4 pieces.

3 Heat the oil in a preheated wok
   and stir-fry the ginger and spring
onions for 1–2 minutes. Add the
mangetout and continue to cook for
1 further minute. Sprinkle the turmeric,
cumin and seasoning over the
vegetables and mix well.

4 Add the crab meat and mussels
   and stir-fry for 1 minute. Stir in
the cooked rice and beansprouts and
stir-fry for 2 minutes, or until hot and
well mixed.

5 Adjust the seasoning to taste and
   serve immediately.

curried crab

serves four

2 tbsp mustard oil

1 tbsp ghee

1 onion, chopped finely

5-cm/2-inch piece fresh root
    ginger, grated

2 garlic cloves, peeled but
    left whole

1 tsp ground turmeric

1 tsp salt

1 tsp chilli powder

2 fresh green chillies, chopped

1 tsp paprika

125 g/4½ oz brown crab meat

350 g/12 oz white crab meat

250 ml/9 fl oz natural yogurt

1 tsp garam masala

cooked basmati rice, to serve

fresh coriander, to garnish

1 Heat the mustard oil in a preheated wok or large, heavy-based frying pan.

2 When it starts to smoke, add the ghee and onion. Stir-fry for 3 minutes over a medium heat until the onion is soft.

3 Stir in the grated ginger and whole garlic cloves.

4 Stir in the turmeric, salt, chilli powder, chillies and paprika.

5 Increase the heat and add the crab meat and yogurt. Simmer, stirring occasionally, for 10 minutes, until the sauce is thickened slightly.

6 Sprinkle in garam masala to taste and stir to mix.

7 Serve hot, over plain basmati rice, garnished with the coriander, either chopped or in sprigs.

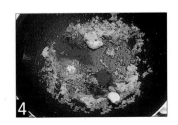

crab fried rice

serves four

150 g/5½ oz long-grain rice

2 tbsp groundnut oil

125 g/4½ oz canned white crab
  meat, drained

1 leek, sliced

150 g/5½ oz beansprouts

2 eggs, beaten

1 tbsp light soy sauce

2 tsp lime juice

1 tsp sesame oil

salt

sliced lime, to garnish

VARIATION

Cooked lobster may be
used instead of the crab for
a really special dish.

---

1 Cook the rice in a saucepan of lightly salted boiling water for 15 minutes. Drain, rinse under cold running water and drain again.

2 Heat the oil in a preheated wok or large, heavy-based frying pan until it is really hot.

3 Add the crab meat, leek and beansprouts to the wok or frying pan and stir-fry for 2–3 minutes. Remove the mixture with a slotted spoon and reserve.

4 Add the eggs to the wok and cook, stirring occasionally, for 2–3 minutes, until they begin to set.

5 Stir the rice and crab meat mixture into the eggs in the wok.

6 Add the soy sauce and lime juice to the mixture in the wok. Cook for 1 minute, stirring to combine. Sprinkle with the sesame oil and toss lightly to mix.

7 Transfer the crab fried rice to a serving dish, garnish with the sliced lime and serve immediately.

baked crab with ginger

serves four

1 large or 2 medium crabs,
    weighing about 750 g/1 lb 10 oz
    in total

2 tbsp Chinese rice wine or
    dry sherry

1 egg, lightly beaten

1 tbsp cornflour

3–4 tbsp vegetable oil

1 tbsp finely chopped fresh
    root ginger

3–4 spring onions, cut into
    short lengths

2 tbsp light soy sauce

1 tsp sugar

about 5 tbsp fish stock or water

½ tsp sesame oil

fresh coriander leaves, to garnish

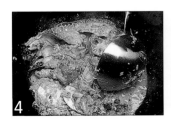

1 Cut the crab in half from the underbelly. Break off the claws and crack them with the back of a cleaver or a large kitchen knife.

2 Discard the legs and crack the shell, breaking it into several pieces. Discard the feathery gills from both sides of the body and the stomach sac. Place the crab meat in a bowl.

3 Mix the wine or sherry, egg and cornflour. Pour the mixture over the crab meat and leave to marinate for 10–15 minutes.

4 Heat the vegetable oil in a preheated wok. Stir-fry the crab meat with the chopped ginger and spring onions for 2–3 minutes.

5 Add the soy sauce, sugar and stock or water, blend well and bring to the boil. Cover and cook for 3–4 minutes, then remove the lid, sprinkle with sesame oil and serve, garnished with coriander leaves.

chinese leaves with mushrooms & crab

serves four

225 g/8 oz shiitake mushrooms

2 tbsp vegetable oil

2 garlic cloves, crushed

6 spring onions, sliced

1 head Chinese leaves, shredded

1 tbsp mild curry paste

6 tbsp coconut milk

200 g/7 oz canned white crab
    meat, drained

1 tsp chilli flakes

1 Using a sharp knife, cut the mushrooms into slices.

2 Heat the vegetable oil in a large preheated wok or heavy-based frying pan.

3 Add the mushrooms and garlic to the wok or frying pan and stir-fry for 3 minutes, or until the mushrooms have softened.

4 Add the spring onions and shredded Chinese leaves to the wok and stir-fry until the leaves have just begin to wilt.

5 Mix together the mild curry paste and coconut milk in a small bowl.

6 Add the curry paste and coconut milk mixture to the wok, together with the crab meat and chilli flakes. Mix thoroughly together.

7 Heat the mixture until the juices start to bubble.

8 Transfer the crab and vegetable stir-fry to warm serving bowls and serve immediately.

mussels in black bean sauce with spinach

serves four

350 g/12 oz leeks

350 g/12 oz cooked, green-
    lipped mussels

1 tsp cumin seeds

2 tbsp vegetable oil

2 garlic cloves, crushed

1 red pepper, deseeded and sliced

50 g/1¾ oz canned bamboo shoots,
    drained and rinsed

175 g/6 oz baby spinach leaves

160 g/5¾ oz jar black bean sauce

COOK'S TIP

If fresh green-lipped mussels are
not available, they can be
bought shelled in cans and jars
from most large supermarkets.

1 Using a sharp knife, trim the leeks
and shred them.

2 Place the cooked green-lipped
mussels in a large bowl, sprinkle
with the cumin seeds and toss well to
coat all over. Leave until required.

3 Heat the vegetable oil in a
preheated wok, swirling the oil
around the base of the wok until it is
really hot.

4 Add the shredded leeks, garlic
and sliced red pepper to the wok
and stir-fry for 5 minutes, or until the
vegetables are tender.

5 Add the bamboo shoots, baby
spinach leaves and cooked green-
lipped mussels to the wok and stir-fry
for about 2 minutes.

6 Pour in the black bean sauce, toss
well to coat all the ingredients in
the sauce and simmer for a few
seconds, stirring occasionally.

7 Transfer the stir-fry to warm
individual serving bowls and
serve immediately.

scallop pancakes

serves four

100 g/3½ oz fine green beans

1 fresh red chilli

450 g/1 lb scallops, without roe

1 egg

3 spring onions, sliced

50 g/1¾ oz rice flour

1 tbsp Thai fish sauce

oil, for frying

salt

sweet chilli dip, to serve

1 Using a sharp knife, trim the green beans and then slice them very thinly.

2 Deseed and very finely chop the red chilli.

3 Bring a small saucepan of lightly salted water to the boil. Add the green beans to the pan and cook for 3–4 minutes, or until just softened.

4 Roughly chop the scallops and place them in a large bowl. Add the cooked beans to the scallops.

5 Mix the egg with the spring onions, rice flour, fish sauce and chilli until well mixed. Add to the scallops and mix well.

6 Heat about 2.5-cm/1-inch of oil in a large preheated wok. Add a ladleful of the mixture to the wok and cook over medium heat for 5 minutes, until golden and set.

7 Remove the pancake from the wok and drain on kitchen paper. Keep warm while cooking the remaining pancake mixture. Serve the pancakes hot with a sweet chilli dip.

seared scallops with butter sauce

serves four

50 g/1 lb fresh scallops, without
   roe, or the same amount of
   frozen scallops, thawed
6 spring onions
2 tbsp vegetable oil
1 fresh green chilli, deseeded
   and sliced
3 tbsp sweet soy sauce
2 tbsp butter, diced

COOK'S TIP

If you buy scallops on the shell,
slide a knife underneath the
membrane to loosen it and cut
off the tough muscle that holds
the scallop to the shell. Discard
the black stomach sac
and intestinal vein.

1 Rinse the scallops thoroughly under cold running water, drain and pat dry with kitchen paper.

2 Carefully slice each scallop in half horizontally.

3 Using a sharp knife, trim and slice the spring onions.

4 Heat the vegetable oil in a large preheated wok or heavy-based frying pan, swirling the oil around the base until it is really hot.

5 Add the sliced green chilli, spring onions and scallops to the wok or pan and stir-fry over a high heat for 4–5 minutes, or until the scallops are just cooked through. If using frozen scallops, be sure not to overcook them as they will easily disintegrate.

6 Add the soy sauce and butter to the scallop stir-fry and heat through until the butter melts.

7 Transfer to warm serving bowls and serve hot.

balti scallops

serves four

750 g/1 lb 10 oz shelled scallops

2 tbsp sunflower oil

2 onions, chopped

3 tomatoes, quartered

2 fresh green chillies, sliced

4 lime wedges, to garnish

MARINADE

3 tbsp chopped fresh coriander

2.5-cm/1-inch piece fresh root
   ginger, grated

1 tsp ground coriander

3 tbsp lemon juice

grated rind of 1 lemon

¼ tsp pepper

½ tsp salt

½ tsp ground cumin

1 garlic clove, crushed

COOK'S TIP

It is best to buy the scallops
fresh in the shell with the roe –
you will need 1.5 kg/3 lb 5 oz.
A fishmonger will clean them
and remove the shell for you.

1 To make the marinade, mix all the
ingredients together in a bowl.

2 Put the scallops into a bowl. Add
the marinade and turn the
scallops until they are well coated.

3 Then cover with clingfilm and
leave to marinate for 1 hour or
overnight in the refrigerator.

4 Heat the oil in a preheated wok,
add the onions and stir-fry for
5 minutes, until softened.

5 Add the tomatoes and chillies and
stir-fry for 1 minute.

6 Add the scallops and stir-fry for
6–8 minutes, until the scallops
are cooked through, but still succulent
and tender inside.

7 Serve immediately, garnished
with lime wedges.

stir-fried squid with black bean sauce

serves four

750 g/1 lb 10 oz squid, cleaned

1 large red pepper, deseeded

85 g/3 oz mangetout

1 head pak choi

3 tbsp black bean sauce

1 tbsp Thai fish sauce

1 tbsp Chinese rice wine

1 tbsp dark soy sauce

1 tsp soft light brown sugar

1 tsp cornflour

1 tbsp water

1 tbsp sunflower oil

1 tsp sesame oil

1 fresh red bird-eye chilli, chopped

1 garlic clove, chopped finely

1 tsp fresh root ginger, grated

2 spring onions, chopped

1 Cut the tentacles from the squid and discard. Cut the body cavities into quarters lengthways. Use the tip of a small sharp knife to score a diamond pattern into the flesh, without cutting all the way through. Pat dry with kitchen paper.

2 Cut the red pepper into long, thin slices. Cut the mangetout in half diagonally. Coarsely shred the pak choi leaves.

3 Mix together the black bean sauce, fish sauce, rice wine, soy sauce and sugar. Blend the cornflour with the water and stir into the other sauce ingredients. Reserve.

4 Heat the sunflower and sesame oil in a preheated wok. Add the chilli, garlic, ginger and spring onions and stir-fry for about 1 minute. Add the pepper and stir-fry for about 2 minutes.

5 Add the squid and stir-fry over a high heat for 1 further minute. Stir in the mangetout and shredded pak choi, and stir fry for 1 further minute, until wilted.

6 Stir in the sauce ingredients and cook, stirring constantly, for about 2 minutes, until the sauce clears and thickens. Serve immediately.

spicy scallops with lime & chilli

serves four

16 large scallops

1 tbsp butter

1 tbsp vegetable oil

1 tsp crushed garlic

1 tsp grated fresh root ginger

1 bunch of spring onions,
    sliced thinly

finely grated rind of 1 lime

1 small fresh red chilli, deseeded
    and very finely chopped

3 tbsp lime juice

TO SERVE

lime wedges

freshly cooked rice

1 Trim the scallops, then wash and pat dry. Separate the corals from the white parts, then slice each white part in half horizontally, making 2 rounds.

COOK'S TIP

If fresh scallops are not available, frozen ones can be used, but make sure they are thoroughly thawed before you cook them.

2 Heat the butter and oil in a wok or frying pan. Add the garlic and ginger and stir-fry for 1 minute without browning. Add the spring onions and stir-fry for 1 further minute.

3 Add the scallops and stir-fry over a high heat for 4–5 minutes. Stir in the lime rind, chilli and lime juice and cook for 1 further minute.

4 Serve the scallops hot, with the juices spooned over them, accompanied by lime wedges and cooked rice.

crispy fried squid with salt & pepper

serves four

450 g/1 lb squid, cleaned

4 tbsp cornflour

1 tsp salt

1 tsp pepper

1 tsp chilli flakes

groundnut oil, for frying

dipping sauce, to serve

COOK'S TIP

To make a dipping sauce, mix together 1 tablespoon each light and dark soy sauce, 2 teaspoons sesame oil, 2 deseeded and finely chopped fresh green chillies, 2 finely chopped spring onions, 1 crushed garlic clove and 1 tablespoon grated fresh root ginger.

1 Using a sharp knife, remove the tentacles from the squid and trim. Slice the bodies down one side and open out to give a flat piece.

2 Score the flat pieces with a criss-cross pattern then cut each piece into 4.

3 Mix together the cornflour, salt, pepper and chilli flakes.

4 Place the salt and pepper mixture in a large polythene bag. Add the squid pieces and shake the bag thoroughly to coat the squid in the flour mixture.

5 Heat about 5-cm/2-inches of groundnut oil in a large preheated wok.

6 Add the squid pieces to the wok, in batches, and stir-fry for about 2 minutes, or until the squid pieces start to curl up. Do not overcook or the squid will become tough.

7 Remove the squid pieces with a slotted spoon, transfer to kitchen paper and drain thoroughly.

8 Transfer the fried squid pieces to serving plates and serve immediately with a dipping sauce.

whole fried fish with soy & ginger

serves four to six

6 dried Chinese mushrooms

3 tbsp rice vinegar

2 tbsp soft light brown sugar

3 tbsp dark soy sauce

7.5-cm/3-inch piece fresh root
   ginger, chopped finely

4 spring onions, sliced diagonally

2 tsp cornflour

2 tbsp lime juice

1 sea bass, about 1 kg/
   2 lb 4 oz, cleaned

4 tbsp plain flour

sunflower oil, for deep-frying

salt and pepper

1 radish, sliced but left whole,
   to garnish

TO SERVE

shredded Chinese leaves

radish slices

1 Soak the dried mushrooms in hot water for about 10 minutes, then drain well, reserving 100 ml/3½ fl oz of the liquid. Thinly slice the mushrooms.

2 Mix the reserved mushroom liquid with the rice vinegar, sugar and soy sauce. Place in a pan with the mushrooms and bring to the boil. Reduce the heat and simmer for 3–4 minutes.

3 Add the ginger and spring onions and simmer for 1 minute. Blend the cornflour and lime juice to a smooth paste, stir into the pan and cook, stirring constantly, for 1–2 minutes, until the sauce thickens. Cover the sauce amd reserve while you cook the fish.

4 Season the sea bass inside and out with plenty of salt and pepper, then dust lightly with flour, shaking off the excess.

5 Heat a 2.5-cm/1-inch depth of oil in a wok to 190°C/375°F or until a cube of bread browns in 30 seconds. Carefully lower the fish into the oil and fry it on one side for approximately 3–4 minutes, until golden. Use two metal spatulas or fish slices to turn the fish carefully and then fry it on the other side for a further 3–4 minutes, until it is golden brown.

6 Lift the fish out of the wok, draining off the excess oil, and place on a serving plate. Heat the sauce until boiling, then spoon it over the fish. Serve immediately, garnished with the sliced whole radish and surrounded by shredded Chinese leaves with sliced radishes.

stir-fried oysters

serves four

225 g/8 oz leeks
350 g/12 oz tofu, drained weight
2 tbsp sunflower oil
350 g/12 oz shelled oysters
2 tbsp fresh lemon juice
1 tsp cornflour
2 tbsp light soy sauce
100 ml/3½ fl oz fish stock
2 tbsp chopped fresh coriander
1 tsp finely grated lemon rind

VARIATION

Shelled clams or mussels
could be used instead of the
oysters, if you prefer.

1 Wash the leeks thoroughly, then trim and slice thinly.

2 Using a sharp knife, cut the tofu into bite-size pieces.

3 Heat the sunflower oil in a large preheated wok or frying pan. Add the leeks to the wok or pan and stir-fry for about 2 minutes.

4 Add the tofu and oysters to the wok or frying pan and stir-fry for 1–2 minutes.

5 Mix together the lemon juice, cornflour, light soy sauce and fish stock in a small bowl, stirring until well blended to a smooth paste.

6 Pour the cornflour mixture into the wok and cook over a medium heat, stirring occasionally, until the juices start to thicken.

7 Transfer to serving bowls and scatter the coriander and lemon rind on top. Serve immediately.

seafood chow mein

serves four

85 g/3 oz squid, cleaned

3–4 fresh scallops

85 g/3 oz raw prawns, peeled

½ egg white, lightly beaten

2tsp cornflour, mixed to a paste
   with 2½ tsp water

275 g/9½ oz egg noodles

5–6 tbsp vegetable oil

2 tbsp light soy sauce

55 g/2 oz mangetout

½ tsp salt

½ tsp sugar

1 tsp Chinese rice wine

2 spring onions,
   shredded finely

a few drops of sesame oil

1 Open up the squid and score
the inside in a criss-cross pattern,
then cut into pieces about the size of
a postage stamp. Soak the squid in a
bowl of boiling water until all the
pieces curl up. Rinse in cold water
and drain.

2 Cut each scallop into 3–4 slices.
Cut the prawns in half
lengthways if large. Mix the scallops
and prawns with the egg white and
cornflour paste.

3 Cook the noodles in boiling
water according to the packet
instructions, then drain and rinse under
cold water. Drain well, then toss with
about 1 tablespoon of oil.

4 Heat 3 tablespoons of oil in a
preheated wok. Add the noodles
and 1 tablespoon of the soy sauce and
stir-fry for 2–3 minutes. Remove to a
large serving dish.

5 Heat the remaining oil in the wok
and add the mangetout and
seafood. Stir-fry for about 2 minutes,
then add the salt, sugar, rice wine,
remaining soy sauce and about half
the spring onions. Blend well and add
a little stock or water if necessary. Pour
the seafood mixture on top of the
noodles and sprinkle with sesame oil.
Garnish with the remaining spring
onions and serve.

seafood stir-fry

serves four

100 g/3½ oz small, thin asparagus
  spears, trimmed
1 tbsp sunflower oil
2.5-cm/1-inch piece fresh root
  ginger, cut into thin strips
1 leek, shredded
2 carrots, cut into matchsticks
100 g/3½ oz baby corn cobs,
  quartered lengthwise
2 tbsp light soy sauce
1 tbsp oyster sauce
1 tsp clear honey
450 g/1 lb cooked, assorted
  shellfish, thawed if frozen
freshly cooked egg noodles,
  to serve
TO GARNISH
4 large cooked prawns
small bunch fresh chives, snipped

1 Bring a small saucepan of water
  to the boil and blanch the
asparagus for 1–2 minutes.

2 Drain the asparagus thoroughly
  and keep warm.

3 Heat the oil in a wok or large
  frying pan and stir-fry the ginger,
leek, carrots and corn cobs for about
3 minutes. Do not allow the vegetables
to brown.

4 Add the soy sauce, oyster sauce
  and honey.

5 Stir in the cooked shellfish
  and continue to stir-fry for
2–3 minutes, until the vegetables are
just tender and the shellfish are
thoroughly heated through. Add the
blanched asparagus and stir-fry for
about 2 minutes.

6 To serve, pile the cooked noodles
  on to 4 warm serving plates and
spoon the seafood and vegetable stir-
fry over them.

7 Garnish with the cooked prawns
  and snipped fresh chives and
serve immediately.

spiced balti seafood

serves four

1 garlic clove, crushed

2 tsp grated fresh root ginger

2 tsp ground coriander

2 tsp ground cumin

½ tsp ground cardamom

¼ tsp chilli powder

2 tbsp tomato purée

5 tbsp water

3 tbsp chopped fresh coriander

500 g/1 lb cooked peeled
   king prawns

2 tbsp oil

2 small onions, sliced

1 fresh green chilli, chopped

salt

1 Put the garlic, grated ginger, ground coriander, cumin, cardamom, chilli powder, tomato purée, 4 tablespoons of the water and 2 tablespoons of the chopped fresh coriander into a bowl. Mix all the ingredients together.

2 Add the prawns to the bowl, cover with clingfilm and leave to marinate for 2 hours.

3 Heat the oil in a preheated wok, add the onions and stir-fry over a medium heat until golden brown.

4 Add the prawns with their marinade and the chilli and stir-fry over a medium heat for 5 minutes. Season to taste with salt, and add the remaining tablespoon of water if the mixture is very dry. Stir-fry over a medium heat for 5 minutes.

5 Serve the prawns (immediately, garnished with the remaining fresh chopped coriander.)

COOK'S TIP
Prawns lose less
flavour if they are put without
water in a tightly covered pan
and set over a high heat to
cook in their own juice.

Vegetarian Dishes

Vegetables play an important role in wok and stir-fry cooking in the Far East and are used extensively in all meals. It is perfectly possible to enjoy a meal from a selection of the following recipes contained in this chapter without meat or fish. Baby corn cobs, Chinese leaves and green beans, young spinach leaves and pak choi can all bring a unique flavour and freshness to a stir-fried dish.

Far Eastern people enjoy their vegetables crisp, so most of the dishes in this chapter are quick to cook, in order to bring out the flavours and textures of the ingredients used. Always buy firm, crisp vegetables, and cook them as soon as possible. Another point to remember is to wash the vegetables just before cutting and to cook them as soon as they have been cut so that the vitamin content is not lost through evaporation.

vegetables with sherry & soy sauce

serves four

2 tbsp sunflower oil

1 red onion, sliced

175 g/6 oz carrots, sliced thinly

175 g/6 oz courgettes,
   sliced diagonally

1 red pepper, deseeded and sliced

1 small head Chinese
   leaves, shredded

150 g/5½ oz beansprouts

225 g/8 oz canned bamboo shoots,
   drained and rinsed

150 g/5½ oz toasted cashew nuts

SAUCE

3 tbsp medium sherry

3 tbsp light soy sauce

1 tsp ground ginger

1 garlic clove, crushed

1 tsp cornflour

1 tbsp tomato purée

VARIATION

Use any mixture of fresh
vegetables that you have to hand
in this very versatile dish.

---

1 Heat the sunflower oil in a large preheated wok.

2 Add the red onion and stir-fry for 2–3 minutes, or until softened.

3 Add the carrots, courgettes and pepper slices to the wok and stir-fry for a further 5 minutes.

4 Add the shredded Chinese leaves, beansprouts and bamboo shoots to the wok and heat through for 2–3 minutes, or until the leaves begin to wilt. Stir in the cashew nuts.

5 Mix the sherry, soy sauce, ginger, garlic, cornflour and tomato purée in a bowl. Pour over the vegetables and toss well. Simmer for 2–3 minutes, or until the juices start to thicken. Serve immediately.

tofu with green peppers & crispy onions

serves four

350 g/12 oz firm tofu,
   drained weight

2 garlic cloves, crushed

4 tbsp dark soy sauce

1 tbsp sweet chilli sauce

6 tbsp sunflower oil

1 onion, sliced

1 green pepper, deseeded and diced

1 tbsp sesame oil

1 Using a sharp knife, cut the tofu into bite-size pieces. Place the tofu in a shallow, non-metallic dish.

2 Mix together the garlic, soy sauce and sweet chilli sauce and drizzle over the tofu. Toss well to coat, cover with clingfilm and marinate for about 20 minutes.

3 Meanwhile, heat the sunflower oil in a large preheated wok.

4 Add the onion to the wok and stir-fry over a high heat until brown and crispy. Remove the onion with a slotted spoon and drain on kitchen paper.

5 Add the tofu to the hot oil and stir-fry for about 5 minutes.

6 Remove all but 1 tablespoon of the sunflower oil from the wok. Add the pepper to the wok and stir-fry for 2–3 minutes, or until softened.

7 Return the tofu and onions to the wok and heat through, stirring occasionally.

8 Drizzle with sesame oil. Transfer the stir-fry to warm serving plates and serve immediately.

green & black bean stir-fry

serves four

225 g/8 oz green beans, sliced

4 shallots, sliced

100 g/3½ oz shiitake mushrooms,
   sliced thinly

1 garlic clove, crushed

1 iceberg lettuce, shredded

1 tsp chilli oil

2 tbsp butter

4 tbsp black bean sauce

COOK'S TIP

If possible, use Chinese green
beans which are tender and can
be eaten whole. They are
available from Chinese stores.

1 Using a sharp knife, slice the
green beans, shallots and
shiitake mushrooms. Crush the garlic
with a pestle and mortar and shred the
iceberg lettuce.

2 Heat the chilli oil and butter
in a large preheated wok or
frying pan.

3 Add the green beans, shallots,
garlic and mushrooms and stir-fry
for 2–3 minutes.

4 Add the shredded lettuce to the
wok or frying pan and stir-fry until
the leaves have wilted.

5 Stir in the black bean sauce and
heat through, tossing gently to
mix, until the sauce is bubbling.

6 Transfer the green and black bean
stir-fry to a warm serving dish
and serve immediately.

mixed vegetables in peanut sauce

serves four

2 carrots

1 small cauliflower, trimmed

2 small heads pak choi

150 g/5½ oz French beans

2 tbsp vegetable oil

1 garlic clove, chopped finely

6 spring onions, sliced

1 tsp chilli paste

2 tbsp soy sauce

2 tbsp Chinese rice wine

4 tbsp smooth peanut butter

3 tbsp coconut milk

COOK'S TIP

It's important to cut the vegetables thinly into pieces of a similar size so that they cook quickly and evenly. Prepare all the vegetables before you start to cook.

1 Cut the carrots diagonally into thin slices. Cut the cauliflower into small florets, then slice the stalk thinly. Thickly slice the pak choi. Cut the beans into 3-cm/1¼-inch lengths.

2 Heat the oil in a preheated wok or large frying pan. Add the garlic and spring onions and stir-fry over a medium heat for 1 minute. Stir in the chilli paste and cook for a few seconds.

3 Add the carrots and cauliflower and stir-fry for 2–3 minutes.

4 Add the pak choi and beans and stir-fry for a further 2 minutes. Stir in the soy sauce and rice wine.

5 Mix the peanut butter with the coconut milk and stir into the pan, then cook, stirring constantly, for a further minute. Serve immediately.

balti dhal

serves four

225 g/8 oz chana dhal or yellow
split peas, washed

½ tsp ground turmeric

1 tsp ground coriander

1 tsp salt

4 curry leaves

2 tbsp sunflower oil

½ tsp asafoetida powder (optional)

1 tsp cumin seeds

2 onions, chopped

2 garlic cloves, crushed

1-cm/½-inch piece of fresh root
ginger, grated

½ tsp garam masala

1 Put the chana dhal or yellow split peas in a large pan and pour in enough water to cover by 2.5-cm/ 1-inch. Bring to the boil and use a spoon to remove the scum that has formed.

2 Add the turmeric, ground coriander, salt and curry leaves. Reduce the heat and simmer for 1 hour, until the chana dhal or yellow split peas are tender, but not mushy. Drain well.

3 Heat the oil in a wok. Add the asafoetida (if using) and stir-fry for 30 seconds.

4 Add the cumin seeds and stir-fry until they start popping.

5 Add the onions and stir-fry for 5 minutes, until golden brown.

6 Add the garlic, ginger, garam masala and chana dhal or yellow split peas and stir-fry for 2 minutes. Serve the Balti dhal immediately as a side dish with a curry meal or leave to cool, then store in the refrigerator for later use.

mixed bean stir-fry

serves four

400 g/14 oz canned red
    kidney beans

400 g/14 oz canned
    cannellini beans

6 spring onions

200 g/7 oz canned pineapple rings

2 tbsp pineapple juice

3–4 pieces of stem ginger

2 tbsp ginger syrup from the jar

thinly pared rind of ½ lime or
    lemon, cut into julienne strips

2 tbsp lime or lemon juice

2 tbsp light soy sauce

1 tsp cornflour

1 tbsp sunflower oil

115 g/4 oz French beans, cut into
    4-cm/1½-inch lengths

225 g/8 oz can bamboo shoots

salt and pepper

1 Drain the kidney and cannellini beans, rinse under cold water and drain again.

2 Cut 4 spring onions into narrow diagonal slices. Thinly slice the remainder and reserve for the garnish.

3 Chop the pineapple and mix with the juice, ginger, and syrup, citrus rind and juice, soy sauce and cornflour.

4 Heat the oil in the wok, swirling it around until really hot. Add the diagonally sliced spring onions and stir-fry for 2 minutes, then add the French beans. Drain and thinly slice the bamboo shoots, add to the pan and continue to stir-fry for 2 minutes.

5 Add the pineapple and ginger mixture and bring just to the boil. Add the canned beans and stir until very hot, about 1–2 minutes.

6 Season to taste with salt and pepper, sprinkle with the reserved chopped spring onions and serve.

chinese vegetable pancakes

serves four

1 tbsp vegetable oil

1 garlic clove, crushed

2.5-cm/1-inch piece of fresh root
   ginger, grated

bunch of spring onions,
   shredded lengthways

100 g/3½ oz mangetout, shredded

225 g/8 oz firm tofu, drained
   weight, cut into
   1-cm/½-inch pieces

2 tbsp dark soy sauce,

2 tbsp hoisin sauce

55 g/2 oz canned bamboo shoots,
   drained and rinsed

55 g/2 oz canned water chestnuts,
   drained, rinsed and sliced

100 g/3½ oz beansprouts

1 small fresh red chilli, deseeded
   and sliced thinly

small bunch of fresh chives

12 soft Chinese pancakes

TO SERVE

shredded Chinese leaves

1 cucumber, sliced

strips of fresh red chilli

dark soy sauce and hoisin sauce,
   for dipping

1 Heat the oil in a preheated wok
or a large frying pan and stir-fry
the garlic and ginger for 1 minute.

2 Add the spring onions,
mangetout, tofu, soy and hoisin
sauces. Stir-fry for 2 minutes.

3 Add the bamboo shoots, water
chestnuts, beansprouts and chilli
to the pan. Stir-fry gently for 2 minutes,
until the vegetables are just tender.

4 Snip the fresh chives into
2.5-cm/1-inch lengths and stir
into the mixture.

5 Heat the pancakes according to
the instructions on the packet and
keep warm.

6 Divide the vegetables and tofu
equally between the pancakes.
Roll up and serve with Chinese leaves,
cucumber, chilli strips, and soy and
hoisin sauces for dipping.

tofu casserole

serves four

450 g/1 lb firm tofu, drained weight

2 tbsp groundnut oil

8 spring onions, cut into batons

2 celery sticks, sliced

125 g/4½ oz broccoli florets

125 g/4½ oz courgettes, sliced

2 garlic cloves, sliced thinly

450 g/1 lb baby spinach leaves

cooked rice, to serve

SAUCE

425 ml/15 fl oz vegetable stock

2 tbsp light soy sauce

3 tbsp hoisin sauce

½ tsp chilli powder

1 tbsp sesame oil

1 Using a sharp knife, cut the tofu into 2.5-cm/1-inch cubes and reserve until required.

2 Heat the groundnut oil in a preheated wok or large, heavy-based frying pan.

3 Add the spring onions, celery, broccoli, courgettes, garlic, spinach and tofu to the wok or frying pan and stir-fry over a medium heat for 3–4 minutes.

4 To make the sauce, mix together the vegetable stock, soy sauce, hoisin sauce, chilli powder and sesame oil in a flameproof casserole and bring to the boil.

5 Add the stir-fried vegetables and tofu to the casserole, reduce the heat, cover and simmer for 10 minutes.

6 Transfer the tofu and vegetable casserole to a warm serving dish and serve with rice.

sweet & sour tofu with vegetables

serves four

2 celery sticks

1 carrot

1 green pepper, deseeded

85 g/3 oz mangetout

2 tbsp vegetable oil

2 garlic cloves, crushed

8 baby corn cobs

115 g/4 oz beansprouts

450 g/1 lb firm tofu, drained, cubed

cooked rice or noodles, to serve

SAUCE

2 tbsp light brown sugar

2 tbsp wine vinegar

225 ml/8 fl oz vegetable stock

1 tsp tomato purée

1 tbsp cornflour

COOK'S TIP

Be careful not to break up the
tofu cubes when stirring.

1 Using a sharp knife, thinly slice the celery, cut the carrot into thin strips, dice the pepper and cut the mangetout in half diagonally.

2 Heat the vegetable oil in a preheated wok until it is almost smoking. Reduce the heat slightly, add the crushed garlic, celery, carrot, pepper, mangetout and baby corn cobs and stir-fry for 3–4 minutes.

3 Add the beansprouts and tofu to the wok and cook for 2 minutes, stirring frequently.

4 To make the sauce, mix the sugar, wine vinegar, stock, tomato purée and cornflour, stirring well to mix. Stir into the wok, bring to the boil and cook, stirring constantly, until the sauce thickens. Continue to cook for 1 minute. Serve with rice or noodles.

tofu & vegetable stir-fry

serves four

175 g/6 oz potatoes, cubed

1 tbsp vegetable oil

1 red onion, sliced

225 g/8 oz tofu, drained weight

2 courgettes, diced

8 canned artichoke hearts, halved

150 ml/5 fl oz passata

1 tbsp sweet chilli sauce

1 tbsp light soy sauce

1 tsp caster sugar

2 tbsp chopped fresh basil

salt and pepper

1 Cook the potatoes in a saucepan of boiling water for 10 minutes. Drain thoroughly and reserve.

2 Heat the vegetable oil in a wok or large frying pan and stir-fry the red onion for 2 minutes, until the onion has softened.

3 Dice the tofu, add to the wok with the courgettes, stir-fry for 3–4 minutes, until begin to brown.

4 Stir the cooked potatoes into the wok or frying pan.

5 Stir in the artichoke hearts, passata, sweet chilli sauce, soy sauce, sugar and basil.

6 Season to taste with salt and pepper and cook for a further 5 minutes, stirring well.

7 Transfer the tofu and vegetable stir-fry to serving dishes and serve immediately.

COOK'S TIP

Canned artichoke hearts should be drained thoroughly and rinsed before use because they often have salt added.

crispy tofu with chilli soy sauce

serves four

300 g/10½ oz firm tofu,
   drained weight

2 tbsp vegetable oil

1 garlic clove, sliced

1 carrot, cut into batons

½ green pepper, deseeded and cut
   into batons

1 fresh red bird-eye chilli, deseeded
   and finely chopped

3 tbsp light soy sauce

1 tbsp lime juice

1 tbsp soft light brown sugar

pickled garlic slices, to
   serve (optional)

1 Pat the tofu dry with kitchen paper. Using a sharp knife, cut into 2-cm/¾-inch cubes.

2 Heat the oil in a preheated wok. Add the garlic and stir-fry over a medium heat for 1 minute. Remove the garlic with a slotted spoon and add the tofu, then fry quickly until well-browned, turning gently to brown on all sides.

3 Lift out the tofu with a slotted spoon, drain well and keep hot. Stir the carrot and green pepper batons into the wok and stir-fry for 1 minute. Spoon the carrot and peppers on to a warmed serving dish and pile the tofu on top.

4 Mix together the chilli, soy sauce, lime juice and sugar, stirring until the sugar is dissolved.

5 Spoon the sauce over the tofu and serve immediately topped with slices of pickled garlic, if you like.

stir-fried ginger mushrooms

serves four

2 tbsp vegetable oil

3 garlic cloves, crushed

1 tbsp Thai red curry paste

½ tsp ground turmeric

425 g/14½ oz canned Chinese straw
   mushrooms, drained and halved

2-cm/¾-inch piece fresh root ginger,
   shredded finely

100 ml/3½ fl oz coconut milk

40 g/1½ oz dried Chinese black
   mushrooms, soaked and drained

1 tbsp lemon juice

1 tbsp light soy sauce

2 tsp sugar

½ tsp salt

8 cherry tomatoes, halved

200 g/7oz firm tofu, drained
   weight, diced

fresh coriander leaves, to garnish

cooked fragrant rice, to serve

1 Heat the oil in a wok or frying
pan and stir-fry the garlic for
about 1 minute. Stir in the curry paste
and turmeric and stir-fry for a further
30 seconds.

2 Stir in the straw mushrooms
and ginger and stir-fry for about
2 minutes. Stir in the coconut milk and
bring to the boil.

3 Slice the Chinese dried black
mushrooms, add to the wok with
the lemon juice, soy sauce, sugar and
salt. Add the tomatoes and tofu and
toss gently to heat through.

4 Sprinkle the coriander leaves
over the mixture and serve
immediately with fragrant rice.

spicy vegetable fritters with sweet chilli dip

serves four

150 g/5½ oz plain flour

1 tsp ground coriander

1 tsp ground cumin

1 tsp ground turmeric

1 tsp salt

½ tsp pepper

2 garlic cloves, chopped finely

3-cm/1¼-inch piece fresh root
  ginger, chopped

2 small fresh green chillies,
  chopped finely

1 tbsp chopped fresh coriander

about 225 ml/8 fl oz water

1 onion, chopped

1 potato, grated coarsely

85 g/3 oz sweetcorn kernels

1 small aubergine, diced

125 g/4½ oz Chinese broccoli, cut
  into short lengths

coconut oil, for deep-frying

SWEET CHILLI DIP

2 fresh red bird-eye chillies,
  chopped finely

4 tbsp caster sugar

4 tbsp rice vinegar

1 tbsp light soy sauce

1 Make the dip by mixing together all the ingredients in a bowl, stirring well until the caster sugar is completely dissolved. Cover the dip with clingfilm and reserve so that the flavours can mingle.

2 To make the fritters, place the flour in a bowl and stir in the ground coriander, cumin, turmeric, salt and pepper. Add the chopped garlic, ginger, chillies and fresh coriander and then stir in just enough cold water to make a thick batter.

3 Add the onion, potato, sweetcorn kernels, aubergine and Chinese broccoli to the batter and stir well to distribute the ingredients evenly.

4 Heat the oil in a wok to 190°C/ 375°F or until a cube of bread browns in 30 seconds. Drop tablespoons of the batter into the hot oil and fry, in batches, until golden and crisp, turning once.

5 Keep the first batches of fried fritters hot in a warm oven while you are cooking the others.

6 Drain the fritters well on absorbent kitchen paper and serve them at once while they are still hot and crispy, accompanied by a bowl of the sweet chilli dip.

COOK'S TIP
Chinese broccoli is also known as Chinese kale and gaai laan. The leaves are green, with a greyish white bloom.

deep-fried courgettes

serves four

450 g/1 lb courgettes
1 egg white
50 g/1¾ oz cornflour
1 tsp salt
1 tsp Chinese five-spice powder
oil, for deep-frying
chilli dip, to serve

VARIATION
Alter the seasoning by using
chilli powder or curry powder
instead of the Chinese five-spice
powder, if you prefer.

---

1 Using a sharp knife, slice the courgettes into thin rings or small, chunky sticks.

2 Place the egg white in a small mixing bowl. Whisk lightly until foamy, using a fork.

3 Mix the cornflour, salt and Chinese five-spice powder together and spread out the mixture on a large plate.

4 Heat the oil for deep-frying in a large preheated wok or frying pan with a heavy base.

5 Dip each piece of courgette into the beaten egg white, then coat in the cornflour and five-spice mixture.

6 Deep-fry the courgettes, in batches, for about 5 minutes, or until pale golden and crispy. Repeat this process with all the remaining courgettes.

7 Remove the courgettes with a slotted spoon and drain well on kitchen paper while deep-frying the remaining courgettes.

8 Transfer the courgettes to serving plates and serve immediately with chilli dip.

2

5

deep-fried chilli corn balls

serves four

6 spring onions, sliced

3 tbsp chopped fresh coriander

225 g/8 oz canned sweetcorn kernels

1 tsp mild chilli powder

1 tbsp sweet chilli sauce, plus extra
   to serve

25 g/1 oz desiccated coconut

1 egg

75 g/2¾ oz polenta

oil, for deep-frying

1 In a large bowl, mix together the spring onions, coriander, sweetcorn kernels, chilli powder, chilli sauce, coconut, egg and polenta until well blended.

2 Cover the bowl with clingfilm and leave to stand for about 10 minutes.

3 Heat the oil for deep-frying in a large preheated wok or frying pan to 190°C/375°F or until a cube of bread browns in 30 seconds.

4 Drop spoonfuls of the chilli and polenta mixture into the hot oil and deep-fry, in batches, for 4–5 minutes, or until crisp and golden.

5 Remove the chilli corn balls with a slotted spoon, transfer to absorbent kitchen paper and drain thoroughly. Keep warm while you cook the remaining batches.

6 Transfer the chilli corn balls to serving plates and serve with extra sweet chilli sauce for dipping.

1

4

5

asparagus & red pepper parcels

serves four

1 red pepper, deseeded

100 g/3½ oz fine tip asparagus

50 g/1¾ oz beansprouts

2 tbsp plum sauce

1 egg yolk

8 sheets filo pastry

oil, for deep-frying

sweet chilli dipping sauce, to serve

1 Slice the red pepper and place with the asparagus and beansprouts in a large mixing bowl.

2 Add the plum sauce to the vegetables and mix until thoroughly mixed.

3 Beat the egg yolk and reserve until required.

4 Spread out the sheets of filo pastry on a work surface and work on them one at a time.

5 Place a little of the asparagus and red pepper filling at the top end of each filo pastry sheet. Brush the edges of the filo pastry with a little of the beaten egg yolk.

6 Roll up the filo pastry, tucking in the ends and enclosing the filling like a spring roll. Repeat with the remaining filo sheets.

7 Heat the oil for deep-frying in a large preheated wok. Carefully cook the parcels, 2 at a time, in the hot oil for 4–5 minutes, or until crisp.

8 Remove the deep-fried parcels with a slotted spoon and drain on kitchen paper.

9 Transfer the parcels to warm individual serving plates, serve immediately with the dipping sauce.

COOK'S TIP

Be sure to use fine-tipped asparagus, as it is more tender than the larger stems.

spinach stir-fry with shiitake & honey

serves four

4 spring onions

3 tbsp groundnut oil

350 g/12 oz shiitake
    mushrooms, sliced

2 garlic cloves, crushed

350 g/12 oz baby spinach leaves

2 tbsp Chinese rice wine or
    dry sherry

2 tbsp clear honey

1 Using a sharp knife, slice the spring onions.

2 Heat the groundnut oil in a large preheated wok or frying pan with a heavy base.

3 Add the shiitake mushrooms to the wok and stir-fry for about 5 minutes, or until the mushrooms have softened.

4 Stir the crushed garlic into the wok or frying pan.

5 Add the baby spinach leaves to the wok or pan and stir-fry for a further 2–3 minutes, or until the spinach leaves have just wilted.

6 Mix together the Chinese rice wine or dry sherry and clear honey in a small bowl, stirring until

thoroughly mixed. Drizzle the wine or sherry and honey mixture over the spinach and heat through, stirring to coat the spinach leaves thoroughly in the glaze.

7 Transfer the spinach and mushroom stir-fry to warm individual serving dishes, sprinkle with the chopped spring onions to garnish and serve immediately.

carrot & orange stir-fry

serves four

2 tbsp sunflower oil

450 g/1 lb carrots, grated

225 g/8 oz leeks, shredded

2 oranges, peeled and segmented

2 tbsp tomato ketchup

1 tbsp demerara sugar

2 tbsp light soy sauce

100 g/3½ oz chopped peanuts,
   to garnish

VARIATION

You could use pineapple
instead of orange, if you prefer.
If using canned pineapple, make
sure that it is in natural juice not
syrup, as syrup will spoil the
fresh taste of this dish.

1 Heat the sunflower oil in a large
preheated wok, swirling it over
the base until very hot.

2 Add the grated carrot and
shredded leeks to the wok and
stir-fry over a medium to high heat for
2–3 minutes, or until the vegetables
have just softened.

3 Lower the heat and add the
orange segments to the wok.
Heat through gently, ensuring that you
do not break up the segments as you
stir the mixture.

4 Mix the tomato ketchup,
demerara sugar and soy sauce
together in a small bowl.

5 Add the tomato and sugar
mixture to the wok and stir-fry
for a further 2 minutes.

6 Transfer the stir-fry to warm
serving bowls and scatter with the
chopped peanuts. Serve immediately.

vegetables with yellow bean sauce

serves four

1 aubergine

salt, for sprinkling

2 tbsp vegetable oil

3 garlic cloves, crushed

4 spring onions, chopped

1 small red pepper, deseeded and
   sliced thinly

4 baby corn cobs,
   halved lengthways

85 g/3 oz mangetout

200 g/7 oz Chinese mustard greens,
   shredded coarsely

425 g/14½ oz canned Chinese
   straw mushrooms, drained

115 g/4 oz beansprouts

2 tbsp Chinese rice wine

2 tbsp yellow bean sauce

2 tbsp dark soy sauce

1 tsp chilli sauce

1 tsp sugar

125 ml/4 fl oz vegetable stock

1 tsp cornflour

2 tsp water

1 Trim the aubergine and cut into 5-cm/2-inch long matchsticks. Place in a colander, sprinkle with salt and leave to drain for 30 minutes. Rinse in cold water and dry with kitchen paper.

2 Heat the oil in a preheated wok or frying pan and stir-fry the garlic, spring onions and pepper over a high heat for 1 minute. Stir in the aubergine pieces and stir-fry for a further minute, or until softened.

3 Stir in the baby corn cobs and mangetout and stir-fry for about 1 minute. Add the mustard greens, mushrooms and beansprouts and stir-fry for 30 seconds.

4 Mix together the rice wine, yellow bean sauce, soy sauce, chilli sauce and sugar and add to the wok or pan with the stock. Bring to the boil, stirring constantly.

5 Blend the cornflour with the water to form a smooth paste. Stir quickly into the wok or pan and cook for 1 minute. Serve immediately.

stir-fried broccoli in hoisin sauce

serves four

400 g/14 oz broccoli

1 tbsp groundnut oil

2 shallots, chopped finely

1 garlic clove, chopped finely

1 tbsp Chinese rice wine or
   dry sherry

5 tbsp hoisin sauce

¼ tsp pepper

1 tsp chilli oil

2 Heat the oil in a preheated wok or large, heavy-based frying pan, swirling it over the base until very hot. Add the shallots and garlic and stir-fry over a medium heat for 1–2 minutes, until golden brown.

3 Add the broccoli florets and stir-fry for 2 minutes. Add the rice wine or sherry and hoisin sauce and stir for 1 further minute.

1 Trim the broccoli and cut into small florets. Blanch in a saucepan of boiling water for about 30 seconds, then drain well.

4 Stir in the pepper and drizzle with a little chilli oil just before serving. Transfer the stir-fry to warm serving plates and serve immediately.

COOK'S TIP

To make chilli oil, tuck fresh red or green chillies into a jar and top up with olive oil or a light vegetable oil. Cover with a lid and leave to infuse the flavour for at least 3 weeks before using.

thai-spiced mushrooms

serves four

8 large, flat mushrooms

3 tbsp sunflower oil

2 tbsp light soy sauce

1 garlic clove, crushed

2-cm/¾-inch piece of fresh galangal
    or root ginger, grated

1 tbsp Thai green curry paste

8 baby corn cobs, sliced

3 spring onions, chopped

115 g/4 oz beansprouts

100 g/3½ oz firm tofu, drained
    weight, diced

2 tsp sesame seeds, toasted

TO SERVE

chopped cucumber

sliced red pepper

1 Remove the stalks from the mushrooms and reserve. Place the caps on a baking sheet. Mix 2 tablespoons of the sunflower oil with 1 tablespoon of the light soy sauce and brush all over the mushroom caps.

2 Cook the mushroom caps under a preheated grill until golden and tender, turning them over once.

3 Chop the mushroom stalks finely. Heat the remaining oil in a preheated wok or heavy-based frying pan, stir-fry the stalks with the garlic and galangal or ginger for 1 minute.

4 Stir in the curry paste, baby corn cobs and spring onions and stir-fry for 1 minute. Add the beansprouts and stir for a further minute.

5 Add the tofu cubes and the remaining soy sauce, then toss lightly to heat through. Spoon the mixture into the mushroom caps, dividing it equally among them.

6 Sprinkle the spiced mushrooms with the sesame seeds to garnish. Serve immediately with chopped cucumber and sliced red pepper.

aubergine & sesame salad

serves four

8 baby aubergines

salt, for sprinkling

2 tsp chilli oil

2 tbsp light soy sauce

1 garlic clove, sliced thinly

1 fresh red bird-eye chilli, deseeded
  and sliced

1 tbsp sunflower oil

1 tsp sesame oil

1 tbsp lime juice

1 tsp soft light brown sugar

1 tbsp chopped fresh mint

1 tbsp sesame seeds, toasted

fresh mint leaves, to garnish

1 Cut the aubergines lengthways into thin slices to within 2.5-cm/1-inch of the stem end. Place in a colander, sprinkling with salt between the slices and leave to drain for about 30 minutes. Rinse under cold running water and pat dry with kitchen paper.

2 Mix the chilli oil and soy sauce in a small bowl and then brush over the aubergines. Cook under a preheated hot grill or barbecue over hot coals, turning them over occasionally and brushing with more chilli oil glaze, for 6–8 minutes, until golden brown and softened. Arrange them on a serving platter.

3 Fry the garlic and chilli in the sunflower oil for 1–2 minutes, until just beginning to brown. Remove from the heat and add the sesame oil, lime juice, brown sugar and any spare chilli oil glaze.

4 Add the chopped mint and spoon the warm dressing over the aubergines.

5 Leave to marinate for about 20 minutes, then sprinkle with toasted sesame seeds. Serve garnished with fresh mint leaves.

chinese mushrooms with deep-fried tofu

serves four

25 g/1 oz dried Chinese mushrooms

450 g/1 lb firm tofu, drained weight

4 tbsp cornflour

oil, for deep-frying

2 garlic cloves, chopped finely

2 tsp grated fresh root ginger

100 g/3½ oz fresh or thawed
   frozen peas

1 Place the Chinese mushrooms in a large bowl. Pour in enough boiling water to cover and leave to stand for about 10 minutes.

2 Meanwhile, cut the tofu into bite-size cubes, using a sharp knife.

3 Place the cornflour in a large mixing bowl.

4 Add the tofu to the bowl and toss in the cornflour until evenly coated.

5 Heat the oil for deep-frying in a large preheated wok.

6 Add the cubes of tofu to the wok, in batches, and deep-fry, for 2–3 minutes, or until golden and crisp. Remove the tofu with a slotted spoon and drain on kitchen paper.

7 Drain off all but 2 tablespoons of oil from the wok. Add the garlic, ginger and Chinese mushrooms to the wok and stir-fry for 2–3 minutes.

8 Return the cooked tofu to the wok and add the peas. Heat through for 1 minute, then serve hot.

broccoli & chinese leaves stir-fry

serves four

450 g/1 lb broccoli florets

2 tbsp sunflower oil

1 onion, sliced

2 garlic cloves, sliced thinly

25 g/1 oz flaked almonds

1 head Chinese leaves, shredded

4 tbsp black bean sauce

1 Bring a large saucepan of water to the boil.

2 Add the broccoli florets to the pan and cook for 1 minute. Drain the broccoli thoroughly.

3 Meanwhile, heat the sunflower oil in a large preheated wok, swirling it over the base.

4 Add the onion and garlic slices to the wok and stir-fry until just beginning to brown.

5 Add the drained broccoli florets and the flaked almonds and stir-fry for a further 2–3 minutes.

6 Add the shredded Chinese leaves to the wok and stir-fry for a further 2 minutes.

7 Stir in the black bean sauce, tossing to coat the vegetables thoroughly and cook until the juices are just beginning to bubble.

8 Transfer the vegetables to warm individual serving bowls and serve immediately.

VARIATION
Use unsalted cashew nuts instead of the almonds, if preferred.

squash with cashews & coriander

serves four

1 kg/2 lb 4 oz butternut
   squash, peeled

3 tbsp groundnut oil

1 onion, sliced

2 garlic cloves, crushed

1 tsp coriander seeds

1 tsp cumin seeds

2 tbsp chopped fresh coriander

150 ml/5 fl oz coconut milk

100 ml/3½ fl oz water

100 g/3½ oz salted cashew nuts

TO GARNISH

freshly grated lime rind

fresh coriander

lime wedges

1 Using a sharp knife, slice the
   butternut squash into small,
bite-size cubes.

2 Heat the groundnut oil in a
   large preheated wok.

3 Add the butternut squash, onion
   and garlic to the wok and stir-fry
for 5 minutes.

4 Stir in the coriander seeds, cumin
   seeds and fresh coriander and
stir-fry for 1 minute.

COOK'S TIP
If you do not have coconut
milk, grate some creamed
coconut into the dish with
the water in step 5.

5 Add the coconut milk and water
   to the wok and bring to the boil.
Lower the heat, cover the wok and
simmer gently for 10–15 minutes, or
until the squash is tender.

6 Add the cashew nuts and stir
   to combine.

7 Transfer to warm serving dishes
   and garnish with freshly grated
lime rind, fresh coriander and lime
wedges. Serve immediately.

leeks with baby corn & yellow bean sauce

serves four

450 g/1 lb leeks

175 g/6 oz baby corn cobs

6 spring onions

3 tbsp groundnut oil

225 g/8 oz Chinese
leaves, shredded

4 tbsp yellow bean sauce

COOK'S TIP

Yellow bean sauce is made from
crushed salted soya beans mixed
with flour and spices.

1 Using a sharp knife, slice the leeks, halve the baby corn cobs and thinly slice the spring onions.

2 Heat the groundnut oil in a large preheated wok or heavy-based frying pan, swirling over the base until hot and smoking.

3 Add the leeks, shredded Chinese leaves and baby corn cobs to the wok or frying pan.

4 Stir-fry the vegetables over a high heat for about 5 minutes, or until the edges of the vegetables are just beginning to brown.

5 Add the spring onions to the wok or frying pan, stirring to combine.

6 Add the yellow bean sauce to the wok or frying pan. Stir-fry the mixture for a further 2 minutes, or until heated through and the vegetables are thoroughly coated in the sauce.

7 Transfer the vegetables to warm dishes and serve immediately.

ginger & mixed vegetable stir-fry

serves four

1 tbsp grated fresh root ginger

1 tsp ground ginger

1 tbsp tomato purée

2 tbsp sunflower oil

1 garlic clove, crushed

2 tbsp light soy sauce

350 g/12 oz Quorn® or soya cubes

225 g/8 oz carrots, sliced

100 g/3½ oz green beans, sliced

4 celery sticks, sliced

1 red pepper, deseeded and sliced

cooked rice, to serve

1 Place the grated fresh root ginger, ground ginger, tomato purée, 1 tablespoon of the sunflower oil, the garlic, soy sauce and Quorn® or soya cubes in a large bowl. Mix well, stirring carefully so that you don't break up the Quorn® or soya cubes. Cover with clingfilm and marinate for 20 minutes.

2 Heat the remaining sunflower oil in a large preheated wok.

3 Add the marinated Quorn® mixture to the wok and stir-fry for about 2 minutes.

4 Add the carrots, green beans, celery and red pepper to the wok and stir-fry for a further 5 minutes.

5 Transfer the stir-fry to warm serving dishes and serve immediately with freshly cooked rice.

COOK'S TIP

Ginger root will keep for several weeks in a cool, dry place. Ginger root can also be kept frozen – break off lumps as needed.

stir-fried peppers with chestnuts & garlic

serves four

225 g/8 oz leeks

oil, for deep-frying

3 tbsp groundnut oil

1 yellow pepper, deseeded
   and diced

1 green pepper, deseeded and diced

1 red pepper, deseeded and diced

200 g/7 oz canned water chestnuts,
   drained and sliced

2 garlic cloves, crushed

3 tbsp light soy sauce

1 To make the garnish, thinly slice
   the leeks into narrow strips, using
a sharp knife.

2 Heat the oil for deep-frying in
   a wok or large, heavy-based
frying pan.

3 Add the sliced leeks to the wok or
   frying pan and deep-fry over a
medium heat for 2–3 minutes, or until
crisp. Reserve until they are required.

4 Drain off and discard the oil, then
   heat the groundnut oil in the wok
or frying pan.

COOK'S TIP

Add 1 tbsp of hoisin sauce
with the soy sauce in step 6
for extra flavour and spice.

5 Add the yellow, green and red
   peppers to the wok and stir-fry
over a high heat for about 5 minutes,
or until they are just beginning to
brown at the edges and to soften.

6 Add the sliced water chestnuts,
   garlic and light soy sauce to the
wok and stir-fry all of the vegetables
for a further 2–3 minutes.

7 Spoon the pepper stir-fry on to
   warm serving plates, garnish
with the leeks and serve.

spiced aubergine stir-fry

serves four

3 tbsp groundnut oil

2 onions, sliced

2 garlic cloves, chopped

2 aubergines, diced

2 fresh red chillies, deseeded and
very finely chopped

2 tbsp demerara sugar

6 spring onions, sliced

3 tbsp mango chutney

oil, for deep-frying

2 garlic cloves, sliced, to garnish

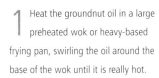

1 Heat the groundnut oil in a large preheated wok or heavy-based frying pan, swirling the oil around the base of the wok until it is really hot.

2 Add the onions and chopped garlic to the wok, stirring well.

3 Add the diced aubergines and chillies to the wok and stir-fry for 5 minutes.

4 Add the demerara sugar, spring onions and mango chutney to the wok, stirring well.

5 Reduce the heat, cover and simmer, stirring from time to time, for 15 minutes, until the aubergines are tender.

6 Transfer the stir-fry to serving bowls and keep warm.

7 Heat the oil for deep-frying in the wok and quickly fry the slices of garlic, until they brown slightly. Garnish the stir-fry with the deep-fried garlic and serve immediately.

COOK'S TIP

The hotness of chillies varies enormously, so use with caution, but as a general guide, the smaller they are, the hotter they will be. The seeds and membrane are the hottest part and are usually discarded.

vegetable stir-fry

serves four

3 tbsp vegetable oil

8 baby onions, halved

1 aubergine, diced

225 g/8 oz courgettes, sliced

225 g/8 oz open-cap
  mushrooms, halved

2 garlic cloves, crushed

400 g/14 oz canned
  chopped tomatoes

2 tbsp sun-dried tomato paste

2 tbsp soy sauce

1 tsp sesame oil

1 tbsp Chinese rice wine or
  dry sherry

pepper

fresh basil leaves, to garnish

COOK'S TIP

Basil has a very strong flavour
which is perfect with vegetables
and Chinese flavourings.
Instead of using basil simply as
a garnish in this dish, try adding
a handful of fresh basil leaves
to the stir-fry in step 4.

1 Heat the vegetable oil in a large
preheated wok or frying pan.

2 Add the baby onions and
aubergine to the wok or frying
pan and stir-fry for 5 minutes, or until
the vegetables are golden and just
beginning to soften.

3 Add the courgettes, mushrooms,
garlic, chopped tomatoes and
sun-dried tomato paste to the wok and
stir-fry for about 5 minutes. Reduce the
heat and simmer for 10 minutes, or
until the vegetables are tender.

4 Add the soy sauce, sesame oil
and rice wine or sherry to the
wok, bring back to the boil and cook
for 1 minute.

5 Season the vegetable stir-fry with
pepper to taste and sprinkle with
the whole fresh basil leaves. Transfer
to a warmed serving dish and serve
the stir-fry immediately.

199

potato stir-fry

serves four

900 g/2 lb waxy potatoes

2 tbsp vegetable oil

1 yellow pepper, deseeded
    and diced

1 red pepper, deseeded and diced

1 carrot, cut into matchsticks

1 courgette, cut into matchsticks

2 garlic cloves, crushed

1 fresh red chilli, deseeded
    and sliced

bunch of spring onions, halved
    lengthways

125 ml/4 fl oz coconut milk

1 tsp chopped lemon grass

2 tsp lime juice

finely grated rind of 1 lime

1 tbsp chopped fresh coriander

COOK'S TIP

Check that the potatoes
are not overcooked in step 2,
otherwise the potato pieces will
disintegrate when they are
stir-fried in the wok.

1 Using a sharp knife, cut the
potatoes into small cubes.

2 Bring a large saucepan of water
to the boil, add the diced
potatoes and par-boil for 5 minutes.
Drain thoroughly.

3 Heat the vegetable oil in a
preheated wok or large frying
pan, swirling the oil around the base of
the wok or pan until it is really hot.

4 Add the potatoes, peppers,
carrot, courgette, garlic and chilli
to the wok and stir-fry the vegetables
for 2–3 minutes.

5 Stir in the spring onions, coconut
milk, lemon grass and lime juice
and stir-fry the mixture for a further
5 minutes.

6 Add the lime rind and chopped
fresh coriander and stir-fry for
1 minute. Serve immediately.

vegetable stir-fry with eggs

serves four

2 eggs

225 g/8 oz carrots

350 g/12 oz white cabbage

2 tbsp vegetable oil

1 red pepper, deseeded and
    sliced thinly

150 g/5½ oz beansprouts

1 tbsp tomato ketchup

2 tbsp light soy sauce

75 g/2¾ oz salted peanuts, chopped

1 Bring a small saucepan of water to the boil. Add the eggs to the pan and cook for about 7 minutes. Remove the eggs from the pan and immediately cool under cold running water for 1 minute. Peel the shell from the eggs and then cut the eggs into quarters. Reserve.

2 Coarsely grate the carrots by hand or in a food processor.

3 Remove any outer leaves from the white cabbage and cut out the stem, then shred the leaves very finely, either with a sharp knife or by using the fine slicing blade on a food processor.

4 Heat the vegetable oil in a large preheated wok or large, heavy-based frying pan.

5 Add the carrots, white cabbage and red pepper to the wok or pan and stir-fry for 3 minutes.

6 Add the beansprouts and stir-fry for 2 minutes.

7 Mix the tomato ketchup and soy sauce in a small bowl and add to the wok or frying pan. Add the chopped peanuts and stir-fry for 1 minute more.

8 Transfer the stir-fry to warm individual serving plates and garnish with the hard-boiled egg quarters. Serve immediately.

pak choi with red onions & cashew nuts

serves four

2 red onions

175 g/6 oz red cabbage

2 tbsp groundnut oil

225 g/8 oz pak choi

2 tbsp plum sauce

100 g/3½ oz roasted cashew nuts

VARIATION

Use unsalted peanuts instead of the cashew nuts, if you prefer. You could substitute Chinese spinach, also known as callaloo, or Chinese flat cabbage for the pak choi.

1 Using a sharp knife, cut the red onions into thin wedges and thinly shred the red cabbage.

2 Heat the groundnut oil in a large preheated wok or heavy-based frying pan until it is really hot.

3 Add the onion wedges to the wok or frying pan and stir-fry for about 5 minutes, or until the onions are just beginning to brown.

4 Add the red cabbage to the wok or pan and stir-fry for a further 5 minutes.

5 Add the pak choi leaves to the wok or frying pan and stir-fry for about 2–3 minutes, or until the leaves have just wilted.

6 Drizzle the plum sauce over the vegetables, toss together until well mixed and heat until the liquid is bubbling.

7 Scatter with the roasted cashew nuts and transfer to warm serving bowls. Serve immediately.

203

nut & vegetable stir-fry

serves four

115 g/4 oz unsalted roasted peanuts

2 tsp hot chilli sauce

175 ml/6 fl oz coconut milk

2 tbsp dark soy sauce

1 tbsp ground coriander

pinch of ground turmeric

1 tbsp dark muscovado sugar

3 tbsp groundnut oil

3–4 shallots, sliced thinly

1 garlic clove, sliced thinly

1–2 fresh red chillies, deseeded and
    finely chopped

1 large carrot, cut into fine strips

1 yellow pepper, deseeded
    and sliced

1 red pepper, deseeded and sliced

1 courgette, cut into fine strips

115 g/4 oz sugar snap
    peas, trimmed

7.5-cm/3-inch piece of cucumber,
    cut into strips

250 g/9 oz oyster mushrooms,

250 g/9 oz canned
    chestnuts, drained

2 tsp grated fresh root ginger

finely grated rind and juice of 1 lime

1 tbsp chopped fresh coriander

salt and pepper

lime slices, to garnish

1 To make the peanut sauce, grind the peanuts in a blender or chop very finely. Put into a small pan with the hot chilli sauce, coconut milk, soy sauce, ground coriander, ground turmeric and dark muscovado sugar. Set over a low heat and simmer gently for 3–4 minutes. Keep warm and leave until required.

2 Heat the oil in a preheated wok or large, heavy-based frying pan. Add the shallots, garlic and chillies stir-fry over a medium heat for 2 minutes.

3 Add the carrot, peppers, courgette and sugar snap peas to the wok or pan and stir-fry for 2 more minutes.

4 Add the cucumber, mushrooms, chestnuts, ginger, lime rind and juice and fresh coriander and stir-fry briskly for about 5 minutes, or until the vegetables are crisp, yet still crunchy. Season to taste with salt and pepper.

5 Divide the stir-fry between 4 warmed serving plates and garnish with slices of lime. Transfer the peanut sauce to a serving bowl and serve immediately with the vegetables.

long beans with tomatoes

serves four

500 g/1 lb 2 oz green beans, cut
into 5-cm/2-inch lengths

2 tbsp vegetable ghee

2.5-cm/1-inch piece of fresh root
ginger, grated

1 garlic clove, crushed

1 tsp ground turmeric

½ tsp cayenne pepper

1 tsp ground coriander

4 tomatoes, peeled, deseeded
and diced

150 ml/5 fl oz vegetable stock

1 Blanch the beans briefly in boiling water, drain, refresh under cold running water and drain again.

2 Melt the ghee in a wok or pan over a moderate heat. Add the grated ginger and crushed garlic, stir and add the turmeric, cayenne and ground coriander. Stir over a low heat for about 1 minute, until fragrant.

3 Add the diced tomatoes, tossing them until they are thoroughly coated in the spice mix.

4 Add the vegetable stock to the wok or pan, bring to the boil and simmer over a medium-high heat, stirring occasionally, for about 10 minutes, until the sauce has reduced and thickened.

5 Add the beans, reduce the heat to moderate and heat through, stirring constantly, for 5 minutes.

6 Transfer to a warmed serving dish and serve immediately.

courgette curry

serves four

6 tbsp vegetable oil

1 onion, chopped finely

3 fresh green chillies, chopped finely

1 tsp finely chopped fresh
    root ginger

1 tsp crushed garlic

1 tsp chilli powder

500 g/1 lb 2 oz courgettes,
    sliced thinly

2 tomatoes, sliced

1 tbsp fresh coriander leaves, plus
    extra to garnish

2 tsp fenugreek seeds

chapatis, to serve

VARIATION

You could use coriander
seeds instead of the fenugreek
seeds, if you prefer.

1 Heat the oil in a wok or large,
heavy-based frying pan. Add the
onion, chillies, ginger, garlic and chilli
powder and stir-fry over a low heat for
about 2–3 minutes, until the onion is
just beginning to soften.

2 Add the courgettes and the
tomatoes and stir-fry over a
medium heat for 5–7 minutes.

3 Add the coriander leaves and
fenugreek seeds to the wok or
pan and stir-fry over a medium heat for
5 minutes, until the vegetables
are tender.

4 Remove the wok or pan from the
heat and transfer the courgette
and fenugreek seed mixture to warmed
serving dishes. Garnish with coriander
leaves and serve hot with chapatis.

green stir-fry

serves four

2 tbsp groundnut oil

2 garlic cloves, crushed

½ tsp ground star anise

1 tsp salt

350 g/12 oz pak choi, shredded

225 g/8 oz baby spinach

25 g/1 oz mangetout

1 celery stick, sliced

1 green pepper, deseeded
   and sliced

50 ml/2 fl oz vegetable stock

1 tsp sesame oil

COOK'S TIP

Star anise is an important
ingredient in Chinese cuisine.
The attractive star-shaped
pods are often used whole to
add a decorative garnish to
dishes. The flavour is similar
to liquorice, but with spicy
undertones and is quite strong.

1 Heat the groundnut oil in a preheated wok or large frying pan, swirling it around the base until it is really hot.

2 Add the crushed garlic and stir-fry over a medium heat for about 30 seconds. Stir in the ground star anise, salt, shredded pak choi, spinach, mangetout, celery and green pepper and stir-fry for 3–4 minutes.

3 Add the vegetable stock, lower the heat, cover the wok or frying pan and simmer for 3–4 minutes. Remove the lid and stir in the sesame oil. Mix thoroughly together.

4 Transfer the green vegetable stir-fry to a warmed serving dish and serve immediately.

seasonal stir-fry

serves four

1 red pepper, deseeded

115 g/4 oz courgettes

115 g/4 oz cauliflower

115 g/4 oz French beans

3 tbsp vegetable oil

a few small slices of fresh
   root ginger

½ tsp salt

½ tsp sugar

1–2 tbsp vegetable stock or
   water (optional)

1 tbsp light soy sauce

a few drops of sesame oil (optional)

1 Using a sharp knife or Chinese cleaver, cut the red pepper into small squares. Thinly slice the courgettes. Trim the cauliflower and divide into small florets, discarding any thick stems. Make sure the vegetables are cut into roughly similar shapes and sizes to ensure that they cook evenly. Trim the French beans, then cut them in half.

2 Heat the vegetable oil in a preheated wok or large, heavy-based frying pan. Add the prepared vegetables with the ginger and stir-fry for about 2 minutes.

3 Add the salt and sugar to the wok or frying pan and continue to stir-fry for 1–2 minutes, adding a little vegetable stock or water if the mixture appears to be too dry. Do not add any liquid unless necessary.

4 Add the light soy sauce and sesame oil (if using) and stir well to coat the vegetables lightly.

5 Transfer the stir-fried vegetables to a warmed serving dish or bowl and serve immediately.

medley of summer vegetables

serves four

225 g/8 oz baby carrots

125 g/4½ oz runner beans or
    French beans

2 courgettes

bunch of large spring onions

bunch of radishes

4 tbsp butter

2 tbsp light olive oil

2 tbsp white wine vinegar

4 tbsp dry white wine

1 tsp caster sugar

1 tbsp chopped fresh tarragon

salt and pepper

fresh tarragon sprigs,
    to garnish

3 Meanwhile, pour the olive oil, vinegar, and white wine into a small saucepan and add the sugar. Place over a low heat, stirring until the sugar has dissolved. Remove the pan from the heat and add the chopped tarragon.

4 When the vegetables are just cooked, pour over the dressing. Stir through, tossing the vegetables well to coat. Season to taste with salt and pepper and then transfer to a warmed serving dish. Garnish with sprigs of fresh tarragon and serve the vegetables immediately.

1 Cut the carrots in half lengthways, slice the beans and courgettes, and halve the spring onions and radishes, so that all the vegetables are cut to even-size pieces.

2 Melt the butter in a wok or large, heavy-based frying pan. When it is foaming, add all the vegetables and stir-fry them over a medium heat until they are tender, but still crisp and firm to the bite.

ginger & orange broccoli

750 g/1 lb 10 oz broccoli

2 thin slices fresh root ginger

2 garlic cloves

1 orange

2 tsp cornflour

1 tbsp light soy sauce

½ tsp sugar

2 tbsp vegetable oil

VARIATION

This dish could be made
with cauliflower, if you prefer,
or a mixture of cauliflower
and broccoli.

---

1 Divide the broccoli into small florets. Peel the stems, using a swivel-blade vegetable peeler, and then cut the stems into thin slices, using a sharp knife.

2 Cut the ginger root into fine slices and slice the garlic.

3 Peel 2 long strips of rind from the orange and cut into thin strips. Place the strips in a bowl, cover with cold water and reserve.

4 Squeeze the juice from the orange and mix with the cornflour, light soy sauce, sugar and 4 tablespoons water in a bowl.

5 Heat the oil in a preheated wok or large frying pan. Add the broccoli stem and stir-fry for 2 minutes.

6 Add the ginger slices, garlic and broccoli florets and stir-fry for a further 3 minutes.

7 Stir the orange and soy sauce sauce mixture into the wok and cook, stirring constantly, until the sauce has thickened and coated the broccoli.

8 Drain the reserved orange rind and stir into the wok. Transfer to a serving dish and serve immediately.

Rice & Noodles

Rice and noodles are staple ingredients in the Far East as they are cheap, plentiful, nutritious and delicious. They are extremely versatile and are therefore always served as part of a meal. Many rice and noodle dishes are served as accompaniments, and others as main dishes mixed with meat, vegetables and fish, all flavoured with fragrant spices and seasonings.

Plain rice is served to accompany a large meal and help settle the stomach between rich, spicy courses. Noodles vary from country to country and are eaten in various forms. Thin egg noodles are made from wheat flour, water and egg and are probably the most common in the Western diet. Available fresh or dried, they require very little cooking and are ideal for quick and easy meals.

chinese fried rice

serves four

700 ml/1¼ pints water

300 g/10½ oz long-grain white rice

2 eggs

4 tsp cold water

3 tbsp sunflower oil

4 spring onions, sliced diagonally

1 red, green or yellow pepper,
    deseeded and thinly sliced

3–4 lean bacon rashers, rinded and
    cut into strips

200 g/7 oz fresh beansprouts

115 g/4 oz frozen peas, thawed

2 tbsp light soy sauce (optional)

salt and pepper

1 Pour the water into a wok with ½ teaspoon of salt and bring to the boil. Rinse the rice in a sieve under cold water until the water runs clear, drain well and add to the boiling water. Stir well, cover the wok tightly with the lid, and simmer for 12–13 minutes. (Don't remove the lid during cooking or the steam will escape and the rice will not be cooked.)

2 Remove the lid, stir the rice and spread out on a large plate or baking tray to cool and dry.

3 Beat each egg separately with salt and pepper and 2 teaspoons of cold water. Heat 1 tablespoon of the oil in the wok, pour in the first egg, swirl it around and cook, undisturbed, until set. Remove to a board and cook the second egg. Cut the omelettes into thin slices.

4 Add the remaining oil to the wok, add the spring onions and pepper and stir-fry for 1–2 minutes. Add the bacon and continue to stir-fry for a further 1–2 minutes. Add the beansprouts and peas and toss together thoroughly. Stir in the soy sauce (if using).

5 Add the rice, season to taste with salt and pepper and stir-fry for about 1 minute, then add the strips of omelette and continue to stir for about 2 minutes, or until the rice is piping hot. Transfer to a warmed serving dish and serve immediately.

chinese risotto

2 tbsp groundnut oil

1 onion, sliced

2 garlic cloves, crushed

1 tsp Chinese five-spice powder

225 g/8 oz Chinese sausage, sliced

225 g/8 oz carrots, diced

1 green pepper, deseeded and diced

275 g/9½ oz risotto rice

850 ml/1½ pints vegetable or
   chicken stock

6 fresh chives

COOK'S TIP

Chinese sausage is highly
flavoured and is made from
chopped pork fat, pork meat and
spices. Use a spicy Portuguese
sausage if Chinese sausage
is unavailable.

1 Heat the groundnut oil in a large
preheated wok or a frying pan
with a heavy base.

2 Add the onion slices, crushed
garlic and Chinese five-spice
powder to the wok or frying pan and
stir-fry for 1 minute.

3 Add the Chinese sausage, carrots
and green pepper to the wok or
pan and stir to combine.

4 Stir in the risotto rice and cook
for 1 minute.

5 Gradually add the vegetable or
chicken stock, a little at a time,
stirring constantly until the liquid has
been completely absorbed and the
rice grains are tender.

6 Snip the chives with a pair of
clean kitchen scissors and stir into
the wok with the last of the stock.

7 Transfer the Chinese risotto to
warm individual serving bowls
and serve immediately.

coconut rice

serves four

275 g/9½ oz long-grain rice

600 ml/1 pint water

½ tsp salt

100 ml/3½ fl oz coconut milk

25 g/1 oz desiccated coconut

fresh coconut shavings to
    garnish (optional)

1 Rinse the rice thoroughly under cold running water until the water runs completely clear.

2 Drain the rice thoroughly in a sieve set over a large bowl. This is to remove some of the starch and to prevent the grains from sticking together during cooking.

3 Place the rice in a large wok with the water.

4 Add the salt and coconut milk to the wok and bring to the boil.

5 Cover the wok with a lid or a lid made of foil, curved into a domed shape and resting on the sides of the wok. Reduce the heat and simmer gently for 10 minutes.

6 Remove the lid and fluff up the rice with a fork. The liquid should be absorbed and the rice grains should be tender. If not, add more water and simmer for a few more minutes, until the liquid has been absorbed.

7 Spoon the rice into a warm serving bowl and scatter with the desiccated coconut. Garnish with the shaved coconut and serve immediately.

> ### COOK'S TIP
> Coconut milk is made from fresh white coconut flesh soaked in water and milk and then squeezed to extract all of the flavour. You can make your own or buy it in cans.

crab congee

225 g/8 oz short-grain rice

1.5 litres/2¾ pints fish stock

½ tsp salt

100 g/3½ oz Chinese sausage,
  sliced thinly

225 g/8 oz white crab meat

6 spring onions, sliced

2 tbsp chopped fresh coriander

black pepper, to serve

COOK'S TIP

Always buy the freshest possible crab meat; fresh is best, although frozen or canned will work for this recipe. In the West, crabs are almost always sold ready-cooked. The crab should feel heavy for its size, and when it is shaken, there should be no sound of water inside.

---

1 Place the short-grain rice in a large preheated wok or frying pan.

2 Add the fish stock to the wok or frying pan and bring to the boil.

3 Reduce the heat, then simmer gently for 1 hour, stirring the mixture occasionally.

4 Add the salt, sliced Chinese sausage, white crab meat, sliced spring onions and chopped fresh coriander to the wok and heat through for about 5 minutes.

5 Add a little more water to the wok if the congee 'porridge' is too thick, stirring well.

6 Transfer the crab congee to warm individual serving bowls, sprinkle with freshly ground black pepper and serve immediately.

stir-fried onion rice with five-spice chicken

serves four

1 tbsp Chinese five-spice powder

2 tbsp cornflour

350 g/12 oz skinless boneless
   chicken breast portions, diced

3 tbsp groundnut oil

1 onion, diced

225 g/8 oz long-grain white rice

½ tsp ground turmeric

600 ml/1 pint chicken stock

2 tbsp snipped fresh chives

COOK'S TIP

Be careful when using turmeric
as it can stain the hands
and clothes a distinctive
shade of yellow.

1 Place the Chinese five-spice powder and cornflour in a large bowl. Add the chicken pieces and toss to coat all over.

2 Heat 2 tablespoons of the groundnut oil in a large preheated wok. Add the chicken pieces to the wok and stir-fry for 5 minutes. Using a slotted spoon, remove the chicken and reserve.

3 Add the remaining groundnut oil to the wok.

4 Add the onion to the wok and stir-fry for 1 minute.

5 Add the rice, turmeric and chicken stock to the wok and gently bring to the boil.

6 Return the chicken pieces to the wok, reduce the heat and simmer for 10 minutes, or until the liquid has been absorbed and the rice is tender.

7 Add the snipped fresh chives, stir to mix and serve hot.

egg fried rice with seven-spice beef

serves four

225 g/8 oz long-grain white rice

600 ml/1 pint water

350 g/12 oz beef fillet

2 tbsp dark soy sauce

2 tbsp tomato ketchup

1 tbsp seven-spice seasoning

2 tbsp groundnut oil

1 onion, diced

225 g/8 oz carrots, diced

100 g/3½ oz frozen peas

2 eggs, beaten

2 tbsp cold water

VARIATION
You can use pork fillet
or chicken instead of the
beef, if you prefer.

1 Rinse the rice under cold running water, then drain thoroughly. Place the rice in a saucepan with the water, bring to the boil, cover and simmer for 12 minutes, until tender. Turn the cooked rice out on to a tray and leave to cool.

2 Using a sharp knife, thinly slice the beef fillet and place in a large, shallow dish.

3 Mix together the soy sauce, tomato ketchup and seven-spice seasoning. Spoon over the beef and toss well to coat.

4 Heat the oil in a preheated wok. Add the slices of beef and stir-fry for 3–4 minutes.

5 Add the onion, carrots and peas to the wok and stir-fry for a further 2–3 minutes. Add the cooked rice to the wok and mix together.

6 Beat the eggs with 2 tablespoons of cold water. Drizzle the egg mixture over the rice and stir-fry for 3–4 minutes, or until the rice is heated through and the egg has set. Transfer the rice and beef to a warm serving bowl and serve immediately.

chinese chicken rice

serves four

350 g/12 oz long-grain white rice

1 tsp ground turmeric

2 tbsp sunflower oil

350 g/12 oz skinless boneless
   chicken thighs, sliced

1 red pepper, deseeded and sliced

1 green pepper, deseeded
   and sliced

1 green chilli, deseeded and
   finely chopped

1 carrot, grated roughly

150 g/5½ oz beansprouts

6 spring onions, sliced, plus extra
   to garnish

2 tbsp light soy sauce

salt

1 Place the rice and turmeric in a large saucepan of lightly salted water and cook until the grains of rice are just tender, about 10 minutes. Drain the rice thoroughly and press out any excess water with kitchen paper.

2 Heat the sunflower oil in a large preheated wok or frying pan.

3 Add the strips of chicken to the wok or frying pan and stir-fry over a high heat until the chicken is just beginning to turn a golden colour.

4 Add the sliced peppers and green chilli to the wok and stir-fry for 2–3 minutes.

5 Add the cooked rice to the wok, a little at a time, tossing well after each addition until well mixed and the grains of rice are separated.

6 Add the carrot, beansprouts and spring onions to the wok and stir-fry for a further 2 minutes.

7 Drizzle with the soy sauce and toss to combine.

8 Transfer the Chinese chicken rice to a warm serving dish, garnish with extra spring onions, if wished, and serve at once.

stir-fried rice with egg strips

serves four

2 tbsp groundnut oil

1 egg, beaten with 1 tsp water

1 garlic clove, chopped finely

1 small onion, chopped finely

1 tbsp Thai red curry paste

250 g/9 oz long-grain rice, cooked

55 g/2 oz cooked peas

1 tbsp Thai fish sauce

2 tbsp tomato ketchup

2 tbsp chopped fresh coriander

TO GARNISH

fresh red chilli flowers

cucumber slices

1 To make chilli flowers for the garnish, hold the stem of each chilli with your fingertips and use a small sharp, pointed knife to cut a slit down the length from near the stem end to the tip. Turn the chilli about a quarter turn and make another cut. Repeat to make a total of 4 cuts, then scrape out the seeds. Cut each 'petal' again, in half or into quarters, to make 8–16. Place the chilli in iced water.

2 Heat about 1 teaspoon of the oil in a wok. Pour in the egg mixture, swirling it to coat the pan evenly and make a thin layer. When set and golden, remove the egg from the pan and roll up. Reserve.

3 Add the remaining oil to the wok and stir-fry the garlic and onion over a medium heat for 1 minute. Add the curry paste, then stir in the rice and peas. Stir until heated through.

4 Stir in the Thai fish sauce, tomato ketchup and chopped fresh coriander. Remove the wok from the heat and pile the rice on to a warmed serving dish.

5 Slice the egg roll into spiral strips, without unrolling, and use to garnish the rice. Add the cucumber slices and chilli flowers. Serve hot.

stir-fried rice with chinese sausage

serves four

350 g/12 oz Chinese sausage

2 tbsp sunflower oil

2 tbsp dark soy sauce

1 onion, sliced

175 g/6 oz carrots, cut
    into matchsticks

175 g/6 oz peas

100 g/3½ oz canned pineapple
    cubes, drained

275 g/9½ oz cooked long-grain rice

1 egg, beaten

1 tbsp chopped fresh parsley

1 Using a sharp knife, thinly slice the Chinese sausage.

2 Heat the sunflower oil in a large preheated wok. Add the sausage to the wok and stir-fry for 5 minutes.

3 Stir in the soy sauce and allow to bubble for about 2–3 minutes, or until syrupy.

4 Add the onion, carrots, peas and pineapple to the wok and stir-fry for a further 3 minutes.

5 Add the cooked rice to the wok and stir-fry the mixture for about 2–3 minutes, or until the rice is completely heated through.

6 Drizzle the beaten egg over the top of the rice and cook, tossing the ingredients in the wok, until the egg sets.

7 Transfer the stir-fried rice to a large, warm serving bowl and sprinkle with plenty of chopped fresh parsley. Serve immediately.

sweet chilli pork fried rice

serves four

450 g/1 lb pork fillet

2 tbsp sunflower oil

2 tbsp sweet chilli sauce, plus extra
    to serve (optional)

1 onion, sliced

175 g/6 oz carrots, cut
    into matchsticks

175 g/6 oz courgettes, cut
    into matchsticks

100 g/3½ oz canned bamboo
    shoots, drained and rinsed

275 g/9½ oz cooked long-grain rice

1 egg, beaten

1 tbsp chopped fresh parsley

COOK'S TIP

For a really quick dish,
add frozen mixed vegetables
to the rice instead of the freshly
prepared vegetables.

1 Using a sharp knife, cut the pork
fillet into thin slices.

2 Heat the sunflower oil in a large
preheated wok or frying pan.

3 Add the pork to the wok and stir-
fry for 5 minutes.

4 Add the chilli sauce to the wok
and allow to bubble, stirring, for
2–3 minutes, or until syrupy.

5 Add the onion, carrots, courgettes
and bamboo shoots to the wok
and stir-fry for a further 3 minutes.

6 Add the cooked rice and stir-fry
for 2–3 minutes, or until the rice
is heated through.

7 Drizzle the beaten egg over the
top of the fried rice and cook,
tossing the ingredients in the wok with
2 spoons, until the egg sets.

8 Scatter with chopped fresh
parsley and serve immediately,
with extra sweet chilli sauce, if desired.

noodle salad with coconut & lime dressing

serves four

225 g/8 oz dried egg noodles

2 tsp sesame oil

1 carrot

115 g/4 oz beansprouts

½ cucumber

2 spring onions, shredded finely

150 g/5½ oz cooked turkey breast
   meat, shredded into thin slivers

DRESSING

5 tbps coconut milk

3 tbsp lime juice

1 tbsp light soy sauce

2 tsp Thai fish sauce

1 tsp chilli oil

1 tsp sugar

2 tbsp chopped fresh coriander

2 tbsp chopped fresh sweet basil

TO GARNISH

peanuts

chopped fresh basil

1 Cook the noodles in boiling water for 4 minutes, or according to the packet instructions. Plunge them into a bowl of cold water to prevent any further cooking, then drain and toss in sesame oil.

2 Use a vegetable peeler to shave off thin ribbons from the carrot. Blanch the ribbons and beansprouts in boiling water for 30 seconds, then plunge into cold water for 30 seconds. Drain well. Shave thin ribbons of cucumber with the vegetable peeler.

3 Place the carrots, beansprouts, cucumber, spring onions and turkey in a large bowl. Add the noodles and toss thoroughly to mix.

4 Place all the dressing ingredients in a screw-top jar and shake vigorously to mix evenly.

5 Add the dressing to the noodle mixture and toss. Pile the salad on to a serving dish. Sprinkle with peanuts and basil. Serve cold.

egg noodles with chicken & oyster sauce

serves four

250 g/9 oz egg noodles

450 g/1 lb boneless chicken thighs

2 tbsp groundnut oil

100 g/3½ oz carrots, sliced

3 tbsp oyster sauce

2 eggs

3 tbsp cold water

VARIATION

Flavour the eggs with soy sauce or hoisin sauce as an alternative to the oyster sauce, if you prefer.

1 Place the egg noodles in a large bowl or dish. Pour enough boiling water over the noodles to cover and leave to stand for 10 minutes.

2 Meanwhile, remove the skin from the chicken thighs. Cut the chicken flesh into small pieces, using a sharp knife.

3 Heat the groundnut oil in a large preheated wok or frying pan, swirling the oil around the base of the wok until it is really hot.

4 Add the pieces of chicken and the carrot slices to the wok and stir-fry for about 5 minutes.

5 Drain the noodles thoroughly. Add the noodles to the wok and stir-fry for a further 2–3 minutes, or until the noodles are heated through.

6 Beat together the oyster sauce, eggs and the water. Drizzle the mixture over the noodles and stir-fry for a further 2–3 minutes, or until the eggs set.

7 Transfer the mixture in the wok to warm serving bowls and serve hot.

ginger chilli beef with crispy noodles

serves four

225 g/8 oz medium egg noodles

350 g/12 oz beef fillet

2 tbsp sunflower oil

1 tsp ground ginger

1 garlic clove, crushed

1 fresh red chilli, deseeded and very
finely chopped

100 g/3½ oz carrots, cut
into matchsticks

6 spring onions, sliced

2 tbsp lime marmalade

2 tbsp dark soy sauce

oil, for deep-frying

1 Place the noodles in a large dish or bowl. Pour over enough boiling water to cover the noodles and leave to stand for about 10 minutes while you stir-fry the rest of the ingredients.

2 Using a sharp knife, thinly slice the beef fillet.

3 Heat the sunflower oil in a large preheated wok or frying pan.

4 Add the beef and ground ginger to the wok or frying pan and stir-fry for about 5 minutes.

5 Add the crushed garlic, chopped red chilli, carrots and spring onions to the wok and stir-fry for a further 2–3 minutes.

6 Add the lime marmalade and soy sauce to the wok and allow to bubble for 2 minutes. Remove the chilli beef and ginger mixture, reserve and keep warm until required.

7 Heat the oil for deep-frying in the wok or frying pan.

8 Drain the noodles thoroughly and pat dry with kitchen paper. Carefully lower the noodles into the hot oil and cook for 2–3 minutes, or until crispy. Drain the noodles on kitchen paper.

9 Divide the noodles between 4 warm serving plates and top with the chilli beef and ginger mixture. Serve immediately.

singapore-style prawn noodles

serves four

250 g/9 oz thin rice noodles

4 tbsp groundnut oil

2 garlic cloves, crushed

2 fresh red chillies, deseeded and
very finely chopped

1 tsp grated fresh root ginger

2 tbsp Madras curry paste

2 tbsp rice wine vinegar

1 tbsp caster sugar

225 g/8 oz cooked ham,
shredded finely

100 g/3½ oz canned water
chestnuts, sliced

100 g/3½ oz mushrooms, sliced

100 g/3½ oz peas

1 red pepper, deseeded and
sliced thinly

100 g/3½ oz cooked peeled prawns

2 large eggs

4 tbsp coconut milk

25 g/1 oz desiccated coconut

2 tbsp chopped fresh coriander

1 Place the rice noodles in a large bowl, cover with boiling water and leave to soak for about 10 minutes. Drain the noodles thoroughly, then toss with 2 tablespoons of groundnut oil.

2 Heat the remaining groundnut oil in a large preheated wok until the oil is really hot.

3 Add the garlic, chillies, ginger, curry paste, rice wine vinegar and caster sugar to the wok and stir-fry for 1 minute.

4 Add the ham, water chestnuts, mushrooms, peas and red pepper to the wok and stir-fry for 5 minutes.

5 Add the noodles and prawns to the wok and stir-fry for 2 minutes.

6 In a small bowl, beat together the eggs and coconut milk. Drizzle over the mixture in the wok and stir-fry until the egg sets.

7 Add the desiccated coconut and chopped fresh coriander to the wok and toss to mix. Transfer the noodles to warm serving dishes and serve immediately.

pad thai noodles

serves four

250 g/9 oz rice stick noodles

3 tbsp groundnut oil

3 garlic cloves, chopped finely

115 g/4 oz pork fillet, cut into
    5-mm/¼-inch pieces

200 g/7 oz cooked peeled prawns

1 tbsp sugar

3 tbsp Thai fish sauce

1 tbsp tomato ketchup

1 tbsp lime juice

2 eggs, beaten

115 g/4 oz beansprouts

TO GARNISH

1 tsp dried red chilli flakes

2 spring onions, thickly sliced

1 Soak the rice noodles in hot water
   for about 10 minutes, or
according to the packet instructions.
Drain thoroughly and reserve.

COOK'S TIP
Drain the rice noodles before
adding them to the wok or
frying pan in step 4, as
excess moisture will spoil the
texture of the dish.

2 Heat the groundnut oil in a wok
   or large frying pan, add the garlic
and stir-fry over a high heat for
30 seconds. Add the pork and stir-fry
for 2–3 minutes, until well browned
all over.

3 Stir in the prawns, then add the
   sugar, fish sauce, ketchup and
lime juice, and continue stir-frying for
a further 30 seconds.

4 Stir in the eggs and stir-fry until
   lightly set. Stir in the noodles,
then add the beansprouts and stir-fry
for a further 30 seconds to cook lightly.

5 Turn out on to a warm serving
   dish and scatter with chilli flakes
and spring onions. Serve hot.

fried rice with prawns

serves four

300 g/10½ oz long-grain rice

2 eggs

4 tsp cold water

3 tbsp sunflower oil

4 spring onions, thinly
   sliced diagonally

1 garlic clove, crushed

125 g/4½ oz closed-cup or button
   mushrooms, sliced thinly

2 tbsp oyster or anchovy sauce

200 g/7 oz canned water chestnuts,
   drained and sliced

250 g/9 oz cooked peeled prawns,
   thawed if frozen

salt and pepper

chopped watercress, to
   garnish (optional)

1 Bring a saucepan of lightly salted water to the boil. Sprinkle in the rice, return to the boil, then reduce the heat and simmer for 15–20 minutes, or until tender. Drain well, rinse with freshly boiled water, then drain again. Keep warm.

2 Beat each egg separately with 2 teaspoons of cold water and salt and pepper.

3 Heat 2 teaspoons of sunflower oil in a wok or large frying pan, swirling it around until really hot. Pour in the first egg, swirl it around and cook undisturbed until set. Remove to a plate or board and repeat with the second egg. Cut the omelettes into 2.5-cm/1-inch squares.

4 Heat the remaining oil in the wok and when really hot add the spring onions and garlic and cook for 1 minute. Add the mushrooms and cook for a further 2 minutes.

5 Stir in the oyster or anchovy sauce and season with salt and pepper, add the water chestnuts and prawns, and stir-fry for 2 minutes.

6 Stir in the cooked rice and stir-fry for 1 minute, then add the omelette squares and stir-fry for a further 1-2 minutes, until piping hot. Serve immediately, garnished with chopped watercress, if liked.

crispy rice noodles

serves four

vegetable oil for deep-frying, plus
   1½ tbsp for stir- frying

200 g/7 oz rice vermicelli noodles

1 onion, chopped finely

4 garlic cloves, chopped finely

1 skinless boneless chicken breast
   portion, chopped finely

2 fresh red bird-eye chillies,
   deseeded and sliced

3 tbsp dried shrimp

4 tbsp dried black mushrooms,
   soaked and thinly sliced

4 spring onions, sliced

3 tbsp lime juice

2 tbsp light soy sauce

2 tbsp Thai fish sauce

2 tbsp rice vinegar

2 tbsp soft light brown sugar

2 eggs, beaten

3 tbsp chopped fresh coriander

spring onion curls, to garnish

1 Heat the oil in a wok or large frying pan and deep-fry the noodles quickly, turning them occasionally, until puffed up, crisp and pale golden brown. Lift on to kitchen paper and drain well. Discard the oil.

2 Heat 1 tablespoon of oil and stir-fry the onion and garlic for 1 minute. Add the chicken and stir-fry for 3 minutes. Add the chillies, dried shrimp, mushrooms and spring onions.

3 Mix together the lime juice, soy sauce, fish sauce, rice vinegar and sugar, then stir into the wok pan and cook for 1 minute. Remove the pan from the heat.

4 Heat the remaining oil in a wide pan and pour in the eggs to coat the base of the pan evenly, making a thin omelette. Cook until set and golden, then turn it over and cook the other side. Turn out and roll up, then slice into long ribbon strips.

5 Toss together the fried noodles, stir-fried ingredients, coriander and omelette strips. Garnish with spring onion curls and serve at once.

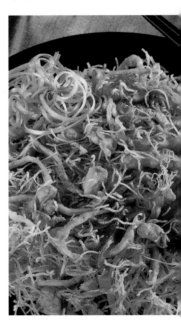

twice-cooked lamb with noodles

serves four

250 g/9 oz egg noodles

450 g/1 lb lamb loin fillet,
    sliced thinly

2 tbsp dark soy sauce

2 tbsp sunflower oil

2 garlic cloves, crushed

1 tbsp caster sugar

2 tbsp oyster sauce

175 g/6 oz baby spinach

COOK'S TIP

If using dried noodles, follow
the instructions on the packet as
they require less soaking.

1 Place the egg noodles in a large bowl and add sufficient boiling water to cover. Leave to soak for about 10 minutes, or according to the packet instructions.

2 Bring a large saucepan of water to the boil. Add the lamb and cook for 5 minutes. Drain thoroughly.

3 Place the slices of lamb in a bowl and mix with the soy sauce and 1 tablespoon of the sunflower oil.

4 Heat the remaining sunflower oil in a large preheated wok, swirling the oil around until it is really hot.

5 Add the marinated lamb and crushed garlic to the wok and stir-fry for about 5 minutes, or until the meat is just beginning to brown.

6 Add the caster sugar and oyster sauce to the wok and stir until thoroughly mixed together.

7 Drain the noodles thoroughly. Add the noodles to the wok and stir-fry for a further 5 minutes.

8 Add the spinach to the wok and cook for 1 minute, or until the leaves just wilt. Transfer the lamb and noodles to serving bowls and serve hot.

chinese vegetable rice

serves four

350 g/12 oz long-grain white rice

1 tsp turmeric

2 tbsp sunflower oil

225 g/8 oz courgettes, sliced

1 red pepper, deseeded and sliced

1 green pepper, deseeded
    and sliced

1 fresh green chilli, deseeded and
    finely chopped

1 carrot, coarsely grated

150 g/5½ oz beansprouts

6 spring onions, sliced, plus extra to
    garnish (optional)

2 tbsp light soy sauce

salt

COOK'S TIP

For real luxury, add a few saffron
threads infused in boiling water
instead of the turmeric.

1 Place the rice and turmeric in a pan of lightly salted water and bring to the boil. Reduce the heat and simmer for about 12–15 minutes, until the rice is just tender. Drain the rice thoroughly and press out any excess water with a sheet of kitchen paper. Leave until required.

2 Heat the sunflower oil in a large preheated wok.

3 Add the courgettes to the wok and stir-fry for about 2 minutes.

4 Add the peppers and chilli to the wok and stir-fry for 2–3 minutes.

5 Add the cooked rice to the wok, a little at a time, tossing well after each addition.

6 Add the carrots, beansprouts and spring onions to the wok and stir-fry for a further 2 minutes.

7 Drizzle with soy sauce and serve at once, garnished with extra spring onions, if desired.

240

thai-style noodle röstis

serves four

125 g/4½ oz vermicelli rice noodles

2 spring onions, shredded finely

1 lemon grass stalk, shredded finely

3 tbsp finely shredded fresh coconut

vegetable oil, for frying

fresh red chillies, to garnish

TO SERVE

115 g/4 oz beansprouts

1 small red onion, sliced thinly

1 avocado, peeled, stoned and
    thinly sliced

2 tbsp lime juice

2 tbsp Chinese rice wine

1 tsp chilli sauce

1 Break the rice noodles into short pieces and soak in hot water for about 4 minutes, or according to the packet instructions. Drain thoroughly and pat dry with kitchen paper.

2 Stir together the noodles, spring onions, lemon grass and coconut.

3 Heat a small amount of oil in a wok or heavy-based frying pan until very hot. Brush the inside of a 9-cm/3½-inch round biscuit cutter with oil and place in the pan. Spoon a small amount of noodle mixture into the cutter just to cover the base of the wok or pan, then press down lightly with the back of a spoon.

4 Fry for 30 seconds, then carefully remove the cutter and continue frying the rösti until it is golden brown, turning it over once with a spatula. Remove the rösti and drain it on absorbent kitchen paper. Repeat with the remaining noodles, to make about 12 röstis.

5 To serve, arrange the noodle röstis in small stacks, with some beansprouts, red onion slices and avocado slices between the layers. Mix the lime juice, rice wine and chilli sauce together and spoon a little over each stack of röstis just before serving, garnished with red chillies.

rice noodles with spinach

serves four

115 g/4 oz thin rice stick noodles

2 tbsp dried shrimp (optional)

250 g/9 oz baby spinach leaves

1 tbsp groundnut oil

2 garlic cloves, chopped finely

2 tsp Thai green curry paste

1 tsp sugar

1 tbsp light soy sauce

COOK'S TIP

It is best to choose young spinach leaves for this dish, as they are beautifully tender and cook within a matter of seconds. If you can only get older spinach, however, shred the leaves before adding to the dish so they cook more quickly.

1 Soak the rice stick noodles in hot water for 15 minutes, or according to the packet instructions, then drain well.

2 Put the dried shrimp (if using) in a small bowl and add sufficient hot water to cover. Leave to soak for 10 minutes, then drain well.

3 Wash the baby spinach leaves, drain well and pat dry with kitchen paper. Remove and discard any tough stalks.

4 Heat the oil in a preheated wok or large, heavy-based frying pan and stir-fry the garlic for 1 minute. Stir in the curry paste and stir-fry for 30 seconds. Stir in the soaked shrimp (if using) and stir-fry for 30 seconds.

5 Add the spinach leaves and stir-fry for 1–2 minutes, until the leaves are just wilted.

6 Stir in the sugar and soy sauce, then add the noodles and toss thoroughly to mix. Transfer to a warm platter and serve immediately.

drunken noodles

serves four

175 g/6 oz rice stick noodles

2 tbsp vegetable oil

1 garlic clove, crushed

2 small fresh green chillies, chopped

1 small onion, sliced thinly

150 g/5½ oz lean pork mince

1 small green pepper, deseeded and
    finely chopped

4 kaffir lime leaves, shredded finely

1 tbsp dark soy sauce

1 tbsp light soy sauce

½ tsp sugar

1 tomato, cut into thin wedges

2 tbsp fresh sweet basil leaves,
    finely shredded, to garnish

TO SERVE

salad leaves

radishes

1 Soak the noodles in hot water for 15 minutes, or according to the packet instructions. Drain well.

2 Heat the oil in a preheated wok and stir-fry the garlic, chillies and onion for 1 minute.

3 Stir in the pork mince and stir-fry over a high heat for a further minute, then add the green pepper and continue stir-frying for a further 2 minutes.

4 Stir in the lime leaves, soy sauces and sugar. Add the noodles and tomato and toss well to heat thoroughly.

5 Sprinkle with the basil and serve with salad leaves and radishes.

COOK'S TIP

Fresh kaffir lime leaves freeze well, so if you buy more than you need, simply tie them in a tightly sealed plastic freezer bag and freeze for up to a month. They can be used straight from the freezer.

chilli shrimp noodles

serves four

2 tbsp light soy sauce

1 tbsp lime or lemon juice

1 tbsp Thai fish sauce

125 g/4½ oz firm tofu,
    drained weight

125 g/4½ oz cellophane noodles

2 tbsp sunflower oil

4 shallots, thinly sliced

2 garlic cloves, crushed

1 fresh small fresh red chilli,
    deseeded and finely chopped

2 celery sticks, sliced thinly

2 carrots, sliced thinly

125 g/4½ oz cooked
    peeled shrimp

55 g/2 oz beansprouts

TO GARNISH

celery leaves

fresh chillies

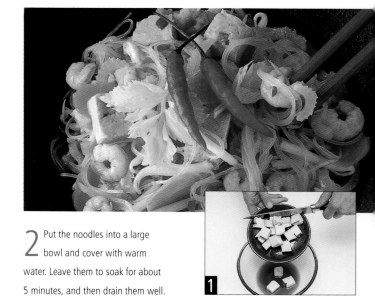

1 Mix together the light soy sauce, lime or lemon juice and fish sauce in a small bowl. Using a sharp knife, cut the tofu into 1–2-cm/½–¾-inch cubes. Add the tofu cubes to the bowl and toss well until they are coated all over in the soy sauce mixture. Cover with clingfilm and leave for about 15 minutes to marinate.

2 Put the noodles into a large bowl and cover with warm water. Leave them to soak for about 5 minutes, and then drain them well.

3 Heat the sunflower oil in a preheated wok or large frying pan. Add the shallots, garlic and red chilli, and stir-fry for 1 minute.

4 Add the sliced celery and carrots to the wok or pan and stir-fry for a further 2–3 minutes.

5 Tip the drained noodles into the wok or frying pan and cook, stirring constantly, for 2 minutes, then add the shrimp, beansprouts and marinated tofu cubes, with the soy

sauce mixture. Cook, stirring frequently, over a medium-high heat for about 2–3 minutes, until heated through.

6 Transfer the noodle mixture to a warm serving dish and garnish with celery leaves and fresh chillies. Serve immediately.

cellophane noodles & prawns

serves four

175 g/6 oz cellophane noodles

1 tbsp vegetable oil

1 garlic clove, crushed

2 tsp grated fresh root ginger

24 raw tiger prawns, peeled

1 red pepper, deseeded and
  sliced thinly

1 green pepper, deseeded and
  sliced thinly

1 onion, chopped

2 tbsp light soy sauce

juice of 1 orange

2 tsp wine vinegar

pinch of brown sugar

150 ml/5 fl oz fish stock

1 tbsp cornflour

2 tsp water

orange slices, to garnish

1 Cook the noodles in a pan of boiling water for 1 minute. Drain well, rinse and then drain again.

2 Heat the oil in a preheated wok. Stir-fry the garlic and ginger for 30 seconds.

3 Add the prawns and stir-fry for 2 minutes. Remove with a slotted spoon and keep warm.

4 Add the peppers and onion to the wok and stir-fry for 2 minutes. Stir in the soy sauce, orange juice, vinegar, sugar and stock. Return the prawns to the wok and cook for 8–10 minutes, until cooked through.

5 Blend the cornflour with the water and stir into the wok. Bring to the boil, add the noodles and cook for 1–2 minutes. Garnish and serve.

stir-fried japanese mushroom noodles

serves four

250 g/9 oz Japanese egg noodles

2 tbsp sunflower oil

1 red onion, sliced

1 garlic clove, crushed

450 g/1 lb mixed mushrooms
  (shiitake, oyster, brown cap),
  wiped and sliced

350 g/12 oz pak choi

2 tbsp sweet sherry

6 tbsp oyster sauce

4 spring onions, sliced

1 tbsp toasted sesame seeds

COOK'S TIP

The variety of mushrooms in
supermarkets has greatly
improved and a good mixture
should be easily obtainable. If
not, use the more common
button and flat mushrooms.

1 Place the Japanese egg noodles in a large bowl. Pour over enough boiling water to cover and leave to soak for 10 minutes.

2 Heat the sunflower oil in a large preheated wok.

3 Add the red onion slices and garlic to the wok and stir-fry for 2–3 minutes, or until softened.

4 Add the mushrooms to the wok and stir-fry for about 5 minutes, or until the mushrooms have softened.

5 Tip the egg noodles into a strainer and drain thoroughly.

6 Add the pak choi, drained noodles, sweet sherry and oyster sauce to the wok. Toss all of the ingredients together to mix and stir-fry for 2–3 minutes, or until the liquid is just bubbling.

7 Transfer the mushroom noodles to warm serving bowls and scatter with sliced spring onions and toasted sesame seeds. Serve immediately.

rice noodles with mushrooms & tofu

serves four

225 g/8 oz rice stick noodles

2 tbsp groundnut oil

1 garlic clove, chopped finely

2-cm/¾-inch piece fresh root ginger,
  chopped finely

4 shallots, sliced thinly

70 g/2½ oz shiitake
  mushrooms, sliced

100 g/3½ oz firm tofu, drained
  weight, cut into small dice

2 tbsp light soy sauce

1 tbsp rice wine

1 tbsp Thai fish sauce

1 tbsp smooth peanut butter

1 tsp chilli sauce

2 tbsp toasted peanuts, chopped

shredded fresh basil leaves, to serve

1 Soak the noodles in hot water for
15 minutes, or according to the
packet instructions. Drain well.

COOK'S TIP

For an easy store-cupboard dish,
replace the fresh shiitake
mushrooms with a can of
well-drained Chinese
straw mushrooms.

2 Heat the oil in a preheated wok.
Add the garlic, ginger and
shallots and stir-fry for 1–2 minutes,
until softened and lightly browned.

3 Add the mushrooms and stir-fry
over a medium heat for a further
2–3 minutes. Stir in the tofu and toss
gently to brown lightly.

4 Mix together the soy sauce, rice
wine, fish sauce, peanut butter
and chilli sauce, then stir into the wok.

5 Stir in the rice noodles and toss to
coat evenly in the sauce. Scatter
with peanuts and shredded basil
leaves and serve hot.

chicken chow mein

serves four

250 g/9 oz medium egg noodles

2 tbsp sunflower oil

275 g/9½ oz cooked chicken breast
portions, shredded

1 garlic clove, chopped finely

1 red pepper, deseeded and
thinly sliced

100 g/3½ oz shiitake
mushrooms, sliced

6 spring onions, sliced

100 g/3½ oz beansprouts

3 tbsp light soy sauce

1 tbsp sesame oil

1 Slightly break up the egg noodles and place in a large bowl or dish. Pour over enough boiling water to cover the noodles and leave to soak for 10 minutes.

2 Heat the sunflower oil in a large preheated wok. Add the shredded chicken, finely chopped garlic, pepper slices, mushrooms, spring onions and beansprouts to the wok and stir-fry for about 5 minutes.

3 Tip the noodles into a strainer and drain thoroughly. Add the noodles to the wok, toss well and stir-fry for a further 5 minutes.

4 Drizzle the soy sauce and sesame oil over the chow mein and toss until well mixed.

5 Transfer the chicken chow mein to warm individual serving bowls and serve immediately.

VARIATION

You can make the chow mein with a selection of vegetables for a vegetarian dish, if you prefer.

251

stir-fried cod & mango with noodles

serves four

250 g/9 oz egg noodles

450 g/1 lb cod fillet, skinned

1 tbsp paprika

2 tbsp sunflower oil

1 red onion, sliced

1 orange pepper, deseeded
and sliced

1 green pepper, deseeded
and sliced

100 g/3½ oz baby corn cobs, halved

1 mango, peeled, stoned and sliced

100 g/3½ oz beansprouts

2 tbsp tomato ketchup

2 tbsp light soy sauce

2 tbsp medium sherry

1 tsp cornflour

1 Place the egg noodles in a large bowl and cover with boiling water. Leave to stand for about 10 minutes.

2 Rinse the cod fillet and pat dry with kitchen paper. Cut the cod flesh into thin strips.

3 Place the cod strips in a large bowl. Add the paprika and toss well to coat the fish.

4 Heat the sunflower oil in a large preheated wok.

5 Add the onion, peppers and baby corn cobs to the wok and stir-fry for about 5 minutes.

6 Add the cod to the wok together with the sliced mango and stir-fry for a further 2–3 minutes, or until the fish is tender.

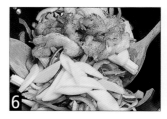

7 Add the beansprouts to the wok and toss to mix thoroughly.

8 Mix together the tomato ketchup, soy sauce, sherry and cornflour in a bowl. Add the mixture to the wok and cook, stirring occasionally, until the juices thicken.

9 Drain the noodles thoroughly and transfer to warm serving bowls. Transfer the cod and mango stir-fry to separate warm serving bowls and serve immediately.